"*Single for a Greater Purpose* is a book that will surely aid the spirituality of those who read it."

—*Cardinal Timothy Dolan*
Archdiocese of New York

"There is a phrase that has become something of a cliche—"a voice for the voiceless"—but it's a phrase that deserves to be revived to help describe what has been achieved in *Single for a Greater Purpose*. I can only guess at the number of dedicated singles who will find in these pages not only lively encouragement but also a depth of insight and spiritual illumination they will find nowhere else."

—*Fr. Paul Murray, O.P.*
or, Pontifical University
of St. Thomas Aquinas

"An important and quite beautiful exploration of an underappreciated state of life, written by one who has lived the single vocation with grace and courage, to the benefit of both Church and society."

—*George Weigel*
Distinguished Senior Fellow and
William E. Simon Chair in Catholic Studies
Ethics and Public Policy Center

"This book is critical. It also happens to be a rigorous, joyful labor of love, and a gift to us. Read it. Pray about it. Discuss it. Guided by it, start looking around and rethinking assumptions and routines. When we pray for vocations and discernment about God's will for a soul, let's be open to the proposal Luanne Zurlo puts forward here—God has put it on her heart for times such as these. Thanks be to God for her hidden joy, and the door she is opening in the Church and the world with this book."

—*Kathryn Jean Lopez*
Senior fellow, National Review Institute
and Editor-at-Large, *National Review*

"The universal call to holiness is a call intended for each one of us. Even to begin answering a call, one must first hear it. Pondering these pages is sure to help a reader to listen better, and to be courageous in finding a way to answer the call by offering something beautiful to the Lord."

—*Joseph W. Koterski, S.J.*
Fordham University, Bronx, New York

"Embracing St Paul's confident hope that 'in everything God works for the good with those who love him,' Luanne Zurlo marks a path for men and women who, for whatever reason, find themselves single but with full hearts for Christ."

—*Fr. Paul N. Check*
Rector, St. John Fisher Seminary
Diocese of Bridgeport

Single for a Greater Purpose

LUANNE D. ZURLO

SINGLE FOR A GREATER PURPOSE

A Hidden Joy in the Catholic Church

SOPHIA INSTITUTE PRESS
Manchester, New Hampshire

Cover by David Ferris Design.

On the cover: Watercolor swallow (553478275) © Eisfrei / Shutterstock.

Imprimatur: ✝ Timothy Michael Cardinal Dolan,
Archbishop of New York, May 6, 2019

Sophia Institute Press
Box 5284, Manchester, NH 03108
1-800-888-9344

www.SophiaInstitute.com

Library of Congress Cataloging-in-Publication Data

Names: Zurlo, Luanne D., author.
Title: Single for a greater purpose : a hidden joy in the Catholic Church / Luanne D. Zurlo.
Description: Manchester, New Hampshire : Sophia Institute Press, [2019] | Includes bibliographical references.
Identifiers: LCCN 2019018424 | ISBN 9781622826568 (pbk. : alk. paper)
Subjects: LCSH: Single people—Religious life. | Single people—Sexual behavior. | Celibacy. | Chastity. | Catholic Church—Doctrines.
Classification: LCC BV4596.S5 Z87 2019 | DDC 248.8/4—dc23
LC record available at https://lccn.loc.gov/2019018424

First printing

To my parents,
who gave me the faith, love, and freedom
that enabled me to discern
God's unique plan for my life

I waited, waited for the Lord;
who bent down and heard my cry,
Drew me out of the pit of destruction,
out of the mud of the swamp,
Set my feet upon rock,
steadied my steps,
And put a new song in my mouth,
a hymn to our God.

—*Psalm 40:1–3*

I will give you treasures out of the darkness,
and riches that have been hidden away,
That you may know that I am the Lord,
the God of Israel, who calls you by your name.

—*Isaiah 45:3*

Launching Ourselves Forward in Love

You have chosen a very strange kind of balance for us,
the kind of balance that can only be achieved and kept
if we are moving,
surging forward with élan. . . .

We have been given a highly precarious state of being,
characterized by complete insecurity.
As soon as we find ourselves examining our life,
it leans over and swerves.
We can only stay upright if we keep moving
launching ourselves forward in an élan of Love.
All the saints who have been given to us as models—
or at least many of them—
seem to have been covered
by comprehensive insurance policies
giving them a kind of spiritual security,
covering them against all manner of risk, sickness,
even spiritual childbirth.
They had official times of prayer,
ways of doing penance, and a whole code
of counsels to bring them
wisdom and defend them.

But we live in our day
in the midst of a crazy liberation;
it is in these circumstances that the adventure
of Your grace is enacted.
You refuse to give us a road map.

Our journey takes place at night.
Each act that we are asked to perform
becomes clear at the precise moment when it is due,
like the illumination of a series of signals.

Often the only thing that we are guaranteed
is the regular weariness
of having the same work to do each day:
the same rooms to clean,
the same faults to correct,
the same blunders to avoid.

But beyond this guarantee everything else
is left to Your imagination
that enjoys having such a good time with us.

—Venerable Madeleine Delbrêl, *We, the Ordinary People of the Streets*

Contents

Appendices

Acknowledgments

If it weren't for Catholic priests, I'd still be an anxious, wandering pilgrim in search of peace and truth. This book is the fruit of years of personal study, prayer, and countless questions posed to a number of patient, holy, and smart priests.

First and foremost, I thank Fr. Wojciech Giertych, O.P., who has been most influential in forming my understanding of the truths of our precious Faith. Fr. Giertych patiently answered my questions, provided me with the framework with which to approach this topic, twice reviewed my manuscript, and nudged me to complete this project. Words cannot express the depth of my appreciation for this beloved Polish priest tucked away behind Vatican walls.

Fr. Paul Murray, O.P., gave me the initial inspiration to write *Single for a Greater Purpose: A Hidden Joy*. Without encouragement from a masterful wordsmith like Fr. Paul, I would not have had the confidence to embark on such a project.

Fr. Carleton Jones, O.P., has been an insightful, caring guide. He has supported me with a masterfully delicate but firm hand. I am deeply grateful and honored to count Fr. Carleton as a dear friend.

I thank Fr. Paul Check, who provided critical feedback on my manuscript and helped to clarify my thinking about the idea of vocation in the Church. I also extend my gratitude to Fr. Gerald

Murray, who helped me to understand pertinent elements of canon law relating to vows and promises, to Fr. Joseph Koterski, S.J., and to Fr. Roger Landry, who also provided key insights.

I am blessed to have a group of dear Catholic friends who provided personal perspectives on various aspects of single life and on the dedicated single vocation in the Catholic Church. Susan Conroy has been a great inspiration to me. Among my closest acquaintances, she was the first to embark upon this relatively untrodden path, clearing the way for others to follow. I also thank Mary Schwarz; Mary Anastasia O'Grady; Darla Romfo; Anna Halpine; Pia, Sonali, and Adele Bruschi; Michelle Viegas; Sophia Aguirre; Therese Bermpohl; Theresa Notare; Susan Toscani; Lylian Peraza; Paula James; Nona Aguilar; Elizabeth Santorum Marcolini; Mary Kiyonaga; Jeanne Smith; Tess O'Dwyer; and Stephanie Saroki de Garcia.

I am grateful also for those unnamed here who shaped my thinking and supported my efforts to understand this hidden, joyful vocation in the Catholic Church.

Foreword

This book begins as an objective reflection—theological, ecclesiological, and also sociological—and ends up being very personal. In this way, it portrays the spiritual journey of the author. In reading it, some may be inclined to judge that it is the work of an unmarried woman, one among many in contemporary society, who is trying to make sense of her life and finally opts for a single life dedicated to God, maybe because a good man was too hard to come by. This is one way of reading this book, and it probably corresponds to the timeline and stages of her discovery of the issues that are reflected upon here. But this is a superficial reading. In truth, this book should be read in reverse sequence because the timeline develops thus: First of all, there is God, who is calling the soul, planning the events of life, arranging things in such a way that some of life's prospects do not work out and other avenues open, suggesting reading material, and enabling encounters with people who can help, nudge on, and explain. Secondarily, there is the individual, who slowly, in time, discovers the Divine Hand. Behind the scenes, God is always in charge, and it is He who is calling in a special way. That is why the final pages of this book, which are so personal, are most important. From the throng of dark and difficult questions, from the sincere pondering, praying, discussing, and reading, finally emerges the plan that God has had all along—a real encounter with the soul, placed in the world but living out the fullness of whatever God has to offer.

As I read this book, I suddenly remembered a sermon preached by Pope Benedict XVI to a group of bishops. They came from a country where the Church was passing through a difficult phase. Benedict XVI told them that everything God did throughout salvation history turned out to be a failure, and yet, in the chaos and bewilderment, God always came up with a better solution. He created the angels, but some rebelled, so He created Adam and Eve, calling them to a special intimacy with Him. When Adam sinned, the plan of salvation was given a new focus. God specially chose Abraham and his descendants to prepare for the coming of His only Son, but throughout the Old Testament they kept forgetting about God and failing to recognize His loving hand. So God sent the prophets, who, more often than not, were rejected. Finally, God sent His Son, but He, too, was rejected and was crucified. It was then that the Church was born and sent to the entire world. Peter went to the capital of the empire, to Rome, but he was rejected there, and so he went to the poor slaves hiding in the catacombs. It was the same throughout Church history. When Europe rebelled in the Reformation, the American continent found the Faith. At every stage, in spite of difficulties, God always came up with a new, surprising, and better way forward.

It seems that now, in the face of difficulties in the world and in the Church, which I need not describe, God is calling for an army of dedicated laity, living in the world with professional lives and lay lifestyles, but nourished from within by a personal encounter with Him alone. The dedicated laity—who are not priests and nuns, who do not wear religious habits, who are within the congregation of an average parish and are true in their total dedication to God—are the leaven of new life. The Church grows from within, from the quality of the spiritual lives of individuals who exercise "faith working through love" (Gal. 5:6) and, more extraordinary still, who support the theological virtues with a total, undivided consecrated life. In this, they receive no prize, no official garment, no special recognition, no respected social role, but just one reward: a hidden, spiritual joy.

—Fr. Wojciech Giertych, O.P.
Theologian of the Papal Household

Single for a Greater Purpose

Introduction

Throughout her history, the Church has been enriched by a small minority who live out their lives in dedicated service to the Kingdom without marrying or entering structured religious communities.

The lay state—especially marriage—has received much attention, and its value has been strongly emphasized since the Second Vatican Council's proclamation of the "universal call to holiness." This importance placed on marriage does not deny the Council of Trent's clear articulation of the objective superiority of celibacy, but it does represent an important shift in emphasis. An underappreciated consequence of this newfound, deserved appreciation for marriage is that the lay state has come to be viewed primarily in terms of the marriage state.

Pastorally, singles have fallen through the cracks. At the same time, the number of singles in society and in the Church has exploded. The U.S. Census Bureau reported in 2015 that 109 million (45 percent of American adults) are unmarried, of whom 69 million (63 percent) have never been married. To compare, in 1950, some 33 percent of American adults were unmarried, 20 million or so having never been married. So today, there are nearly 50 million *more* American adults who are single and never married than there were two generations ago.

Reasons for the dramatic increase in singles are thought generally to fall into two camps, moral and economic. The moral explanation goes something like this: a disintegration of sexual mores throughout society (and the rejection of *Humanae Vitae* by many Catholic laity and clergy), combined with a materialistic, consumerist, self-centered mind-set, has led many to forgo marriage, children, and the inherent sacrifices of family life, in exchange for libertine lives of so-called freedom.

The economic explanation might be summed up like this: in the aggregate, men are falling behind financially, and, without well-paying jobs, they make poor marriage material; and now that women have better professional opportunities, the economic incentive to marry has been greatly reduced, even for those who want children.

There is a third, less talked about spiritual explanation for the dramatic rise in singles. The breakdown of the family and the moral disintegration of culture has spawned great numbers of poorly formed, wounded souls who are psychologically and spiritually unable to enter into true sacramental marriages. In an astute observation, a friend likened the lack of marriage-formed people today to the periods after World War I and World War II, which witnessed a sudden spike in single women due to the high war casualties.

Could there be another positive, transcendent reason for the increase of singles? Might God be calling more Catholics to a deeper communion with Him, to live as lay celibates and bring gospel values to a sex-crazed, increasingly secularized culture? Words and facts have become devalued in our media-saturated culture. What catches the attention of a distracted world are lives authentically and joyfully lived. How powerful is the witness of men and women who forgo what society places such a high premium on, namely, sex, in order to bind themselves more fully and exclusively to

Jesus Christ, leading sacrificial, yet creative lives of joy and élan in today's secular world!

Priests and religious have historically played this witness role. But people tend to imitate what is closer and more familiar to them. In light of the rapid growth of unchurched men and women (35 percent of today's millennials), might joyful, dedicated singles living outwardly "normal" lives, woven into the fabric of secular life, serve as relevant witnesses to many parts of our culture? Does a post-Christian society have a greater need of hidden vocations, hearkening back to the early years of the Church?

To speculate further, might God be calling more people to lay celibacy in order to serve as spiritual warriors against the prevailing sin of the day, impurity? Once the Christian persecutions died down after Emperor Constantine's conversion, St. Gregory the Great taught that chastity served as a substitute for martyrdom:

> Now, though the era of persecution is gone, yet our peace has its martyrdom, because though we bend not the neck to the sword, yet with a spiritual weapon we slay fleshly desires in our hearts. Hence a chastity dedicated to God demands strong and noble souls, souls ready to do battle and conquer "for the sake of the kingdom of heaven."[1]

There has been a fair amount of discussion in recent years as to whether there is a single lay vocation in the eyes of the Church. Singles do not occupy a formal, canonically designated state as do couples living in the state of marriage or as ordained or vowed men and women living in clerical or religious states do. Formal vocations as defined by the Church have traditionally and canonically

[1] St. Gregory M., *Hom. in Evang.*, bk. I, hom. 3, no. 4; PL LXXVI, 1089, quoted in Pius XII, Encyclical *Sacra Virginitas* (March 25, 1954), no. 49.

meant one of these permanent states of life. But vocation can also be understood in broader terms.

Some who refute the existence of a vocational call to live as a single layperson suggest that singles have either missed their vocation to the priesthood or religious life or are too picky, selfish, or undesirable to get married. Whether it is God's permissive or active will that so many in the Church today are single is not the point. Our most important vocation is to love and serve God, and we do so by living in hope, allowing ourselves to be led by God irrespective of our state of life. This daily responsiveness to divine calls is a true Christian vocation and one based upon the graces of baptism. Living in a state of anxiety, waiting for something better to come along, means that, deep down, one has not truly accepted being led by God. Whether one is *called* to be single or one is single *by circumstance* is irrelevant to the fact that *all* of us, through baptism and confirmation, are given the graces to become saints.

With the pastoral sensitivity, clarity, and practicality for which he is known, St. Francis de Sales defines a true vocation as:

> nothing other than the firm and constant will possessed by the person called, to want to serve God in the manner and in the place where the Divine Majesty calls her. This is the best mark one could have to know when a vocation is true.[2]

According to de Sales, a true vocation consists of three elements: constancy, a desire to love and serve God, and an embrace

[2] St. Francis de Sales, "*Les vrays entretiens spirituels*," quoted in Joseph Bolin, *Paths of Love: The Discernment of Vocation according to the Teaching of Aquinas, Ignatius, and Pope John Paul II* (self-pub., CreateSpace, 2008), 37.

of the circumstances in which God calls us. Vocation can also be thought of as a gift, a response to God's love for us by the gifting of ourselves to another: "Man, who is the only creature on earth which God willed for itself, cannot fully find himself except through a sincere gift of himself."[3] True gifts are long-lasting, freely and joyfully given, and appropriate to our particular circumstances.

Formal, canonically defined vocations to the priestly, religious, or married states entail a permanent, loving gift of self, directed to God, or to God and also a spouse and family, normally expressed publicly. Lay singles called to live celibate lives can love Christ in an unencumbered, creative way amid the secular world. Those who have discerned that God is calling them to Himself and who choose to respond by freely giving themselves permanently and exclusively to Him may express this through private vows, promises, or personal commitments. Due to our natural emotions, making a commitment in the presence of a trusted priest or spiritual director, even if private, helps one persevere and offers mental stability. This is not a formal vocation as traditionally understood by the Church, but, for many, it is a vocational call from God within the lay state.

The dedicated single life is a vocation that is hidden and little understood, if not devalued, not only by broader society, but also by many Catholics, including priests and religious. Indeed, most people feel a bit sorry for single, faithful Catholics, even those called to this unique vocation. For many, it is not a life that was planned for or dreamed of. Many discern that Jesus Christ called them to Himself later in life, often after disappointments. In an address to the women of Italy, delivered in war-ravished Europe in October 1945, Pope Pius XII said:

[3] Second Vatican Council, Pastoral Council on the Church in the Modern World *Gaudium et Spes* (December 7, 1965), no. 24.

> When one thinks upon the maidens and the women who voluntarily renounce marriage in order to consecrate themselves to a higher life of contemplation, of sacrifice, and of charity, a luminous word comes immediately to the lips: vocation! ... This vocation, this call of love, makes itself felt in very diverse manners.... But, also, the young Christian woman, remaining unmarried in spite of herself, who nevertheless trusts in the providence of the heavenly Father, recognizes in the vicissitudes of life the voice of the Master: "*Magister adest et vocat te*" (John 11:28); "It is the Master, and He is calling you!" She responds, she renounces the beloved dream of her adolescence and her youth; to have a faithful companion in life, to form a family! And in the impossibility of marriage she recognizes her vocation; then, with a broken but submissive heart, she also gives her whole self to more noble and diverse good works.[4]

Celibacy has traditionally been viewed as a more spiritually fruitful way of living one's life. Theological writings throughout the ages beautifully describe the fecundity of celibacy. I believe that the humble nature of lay celibacy gives this vocation the potential to be exceedingly fruitful. If someone asked me to pick a patron saint of dedicated lay singles, it would be Simon of Cyrene. Compelled by the Romans to help Jesus carry His Cross, Simon at first resisted this extraordinarily privileged call to walk at Jesus' side, alone, just he and Jesus. But then, after some moments struggling shoulder to shoulder with Jesus, Simon came to embrace the Cross wholeheartedly and to love Jesus in a personal, uniquely ordered way.

[4] Pope Pius XII, Address to Italian Women, October 21, 1945, AAS 37 (1945), 287.

Much of what is written about Catholic singles has a "woe is me" or "how to be joyful while waiting for the right one to come along" tenor. Indeed, even Pope Pius XII strikes a doleful note in his address to women. As a Catholic who has discerned, after many years, that God had been calling me quietly, but persistently, to be His own as a lay single, I hadn't come across much that spoke positively and directly to this vocation—despite the fact that Holy Scripture and Church history are filled with extraordinary single laity exclusively dedicated to God. Indeed, I know many outstanding persons, especially women, who have discerned, or are discerning, celibate vocations exclusively committed to Jesus Christ in the secular world.

Sadly, I also know of untold numbers of Catholic singles who feel bereft, directionless, unwelcome, misunderstood, and even scorned. Pope Francis speaks often about the need to reach out to the peripheries; there may be no existential periphery greater than that inhabited by many single Catholics. More attention needs to be paid to what God is creating amid the rubble of our troubled, post-Christian world—holy, creative souls who love His Church and are receptive to His grace. These are God's "free agents," so to speak.

St. Thérèse of Lisieux, possibly the greatest theologian of the modern Church, prayed, "I beg You to cast Your Divine Glance upon a great number of *little* souls. I beg You to choose a legion of *little* Victims worthy of your LOVE!"[5] In an age when technology has made humans increasingly powerful, able to control so much in the world, might God be organizing a legion of little, hidden souls who, having experienced His love, are quietly waging a supernatural battle here below? We know that "where sin increased, grace overflowed all the more" (Rom. 5:20).

[5] St. Thérèse of Lisieux, *Story of a Soul*, trans. John Clarke (Washington, D.C.: Institute of Carmelite Studies, 1976), 200.

I spent years asking God to send me a spouse like St. Joseph; then I prayed for patience, then holy indifference, and then that I might embrace God's will for my life, rather than my own will. It finally became clear to me that Jesus was calling me to Himself. Now my prayers are filled with heartfelt thanks. I thank God over and over for this privileged, joy-filled vocation, and I count myself extraordinarily blessed. Through it all, it was Jesus who had the greatest patience with *me*.

Those who have fully embraced the dedicated single vocation are among the most joyful and peaceful people I know. They also tend to be contemplative. Discerning the Holy Spirit's promptings when one need not be obedient to a superior in a religious community or to a bishop or to the demands of a spouse and family requires much prayer, particularly contemplative prayer.

Pastoral outreach to singles involves assisting them in understanding the beautiful call of baptism and helping them to find their unique place in the Body of Christ, the Church. What those who have, or are discerning, vocations to lay celibacy need are *not* more parish singles events. The moment is ripe for more thoughtful theological, canonical, and pastoral work to address the explosion of singles and, more specifically, the under-the-radar growth of dedicated singles in today's world—perhaps like the work that brought about the canonical recognition of secular institutes and the Opus Dei Prelature in the twentieth century. A greater understanding and appreciation of the spiritually rich and fruitful nature of generously lived lay celibacy could also underpin a fuller pastoral response to those with same-sex attractions, the divorced, and the widowed.

Many dedicated, or vowed, singles have time and highly honed skills that the institutional Church could embrace more enthusiastically. Perhaps more importantly, many also have a special calling to pray for and support priests. Furthermore, the Church needs to address in greater depth friendships, which have an important place in the lives of most single laypersons. Given the relatively unstructured nature of the dedicated single vocation, good spiritual direction is important for this vocation to be lived fruitfully. My hope is that this modest book might, in some small manner, encourage readers to address systematically a hidden, underappreciated vocation.

This was the original inspiration behind putting some thoughts to paper. The following words from a beloved Dominican preacher provided the concrete encouragement I needed to embark on this project: "Are you planning a new book, perhaps? I do think you should write more. The talent is not given to everyone, and today's Gospel is all about not hiding your light!"

I am neither a theologian nor a professional writer. I am an entrepreneurial professional in the finance field and a curious, tenacious seeker of truth. Another beloved Dominican preacher, who clarified for me the vocational nature of dedicated single vocations, insightfully, if not bluntly, suggested that my quest to understand and write about dedicated single Catholics was, at its root, a search to understand how I personally arrived at this vocation. He was correct.

—Luanne D. Zurlo
January 21, 2019
Feast of Saint Agnes

Chapter 1

Our Most Important Vocation

The task of the whole of our earthly existence is to bring about what baptism inaugurates.[6]

We are children of God, and if children, then heirs, heirs of God and joint heirs with Christ.

—Romans 8:16–17

What baptism inaugurates is absolutely extraordinary—life as children and heirs of a loving, generous, all-powerful Father and King! Baptism opens up the possibility of eternal joy beyond our imagining. To realize this possibility, our response, as uniquely created and individually chosen heirs, must be to live our lives with God as our primary love and value. This is our fundamental, most important vocation as baptized Christians, which informs the way we live out our secondary vocation, whether as priests, religious, or laity.

One of the most important teachings of the Second Vatican Council was to renew the emphasis on our common vocation as baptized Christians—a belief firmly held in the early Church. The foundational importance of baptism is gradually becoming more

[6] Columba Marmion, *Christ, The Life of the Soul* (Bethesda, MD: Zaccheus Press, 2005), 210.

appreciated again, but the tenor of the discussion surrounding legitimate vocations and single people in the Church still reflects a general underappreciation of this extraordinary, undeserved gift from our Father, who loves us with abandon and ardently seeks our freely given love in return. We were not baptized by accident; each of us has been particularly chosen and known by God even before Creation.

Also underappreciated, or altogether unknown by many, is the wonderful truth that our baptismal consecration makes us a "chosen race, a royal priesthood, a holy nation, a people of his own" (1 Pet. 2:9). Just as an ordained priest offers Mass *in persona Christi* (in the person of Christ), we laity also offer ourselves to God *in persona sua* (in our own name). Not only does the priest offer himself at Mass as he offers Christ to the Heavenly Father; we all do. This privileged responsibility

> demands that we ourselves be drawn into the sacred offering of Christ Himself. The Passion of Christ must be allowed entry into our own desires, so that we long for this offering with Him at Mass. We are to be "given up" and "poured out," just as Christ Himself is at each Mass. [7]

This powerful, sacred reality hit home with me during a Mass at which both the congregation and the priest faced in the same direction, *ad orientem*. Not only did the priest show great reverence, but so did the congregation. The reality of Christ's concealed presence was made palpable by the comportment of all those offering Mass. I felt more, not less, connected to my fellow congregants and the priest when we all faced forward. In Leonardo da Vinci's painting *The Last Supper*, I used to consider the placement of Jesus and His

[7] Fr. Donald Haggerty, *Conversion: Spiritual Insights* (San Francisco: Ignatius Press, 2017), 213.

apostles on the same side of the table, all facing the same direction, as a compositional device. No longer. Their placement conveys the profound theological truth that, as baptized Christians, we are *all* part of Christ's sacrificial offering to God, our mutual Father.[8]

[8] What a profoundly different experience it is to participate in a Mass celebrated in a church in the round, where one is forced to look at others' faces on the opposite side of the altar, which feeds a distracted and wondering mind—at least it does mine.

Chapter 2

Vocation versus State of Life

We know that all things work for good for those who love God, who are called according to His purpose.

—Romans 8:28

Therefore, that I might not become too elated, a thorn in the flesh was given to me, an angel of Satan, to beat me, to keep me from being too elated. Three times I begged the Lord about this, that it might leave me, but He said to me, 'My grace is sufficient for you, for power is made perfect in weakness.' I will rather boast most gladly of my weaknesses, in order that the power of Christ may dwell with me.

—2 Corinthians 12:7–9

Whether there is a single lay vocation is a question fraught with emotion, as the comments section of any article having to do with single people in the Church reveals. It is a raw, sensitive topic because there are many hurt single souls, wounded by our culture or uncertain about God's providential plan for them. It is a discussion in which people often seem to talk past one another because there is a lack of precision and clarity regarding vocabulary and especially regarding the nature of vocation. Further, today's fluid society—where rigid, sometimes predetermined roles have been replaced by perpetual self-invention—seems to have generated a hunger for clearly labeled identities with respect to one's place in the institutional Church.

Is the question of whether there is an authentic single vocation simply a technical issue of nomenclature, or is there something fundamental to this inquiry that gets at the core of what it means to be holy? I think it is both.

"Vocation" means different things to different people, especially depending on the context. I think what most confuses the discussion is the fact that "vocation" has a different meaning from "state of life," though they are often used interchangeably. The indiscriminate intermingling of these terms greatly muddles the debate.

The word "state" comes from a German word meaning "stand," conveying a static quality. "State," therefore refers to a legal, publicly recognized way of life. "State of life" implies rules of life, established norms and obligations. Throughout most of human history, one's place in society generally was rigidly circumscribed and most often based on birth. During the Middle Ages, the various states included nobles, gentry, serfs, and craftsmen, each having its own officially recognized status. Church-defined ordained or consecrated states were also institutionalized by the Middle Ages. The clergy, for example, had the right to function according to canon law and, in the case of vowed priests, religious rules.

The early Church distinguished between two states of life: ordained (or priestly) and lay, with the lay state expressing itself in myriad, evolving forms over the centuries. The earliest seeds of a third state of life, consecrated religious, were first planted by young Christian virgins (and martyrs) during the first centuries after the foundation of the Church. Consecrated life became more prominent among the early Christian hermits, ascetics, and monks starting around the fourth century, after the early persecution of the Church ended, and especially after St. Benedict's establishment of the rule of monastic life in the early sixth century.

Vocation versus State of Life

During the Middle Ages, professing vows of poverty and obedience, in addition to the long-established vow of celibacy, became the norm for entrance into religious life. It was also at this time that the three states of life—ordained, religious, and lay—became widely recognized. The Church has traditionally viewed those who profess the evangelical counsels, especially celibacy, as having a special, higher calling than those living in the lay state. Indeed, ordained and religious states were commonly referred to as "states of perfection" or "states of election."

The concept of "state of life" is important for understanding the Catholic Church's perspective on the visible, concrete path on which God has placed each of us so that we may best fulfill our particular vocations to love. A state of life in the Church is an objective, public structure, within which people receive the grace to grow in faith, hope, and love by fulfilling sacred vows, either baptismal, consecrated, or marital. We are each called to a state of life that corresponds to our God-given talents and particular life circumstances.

The idea that God calls each of us to a particular state of life is as old as the Church, but it may seem a bit foreign to us today. Societies have become much more fluid, especially here in the United States, which was founded on the notion that one's status at birth, whether lowly or noble, need not determine one's earthly destiny. And, over the ages, some have pushed back against extreme ways in which the evangelical counsels were lived out and against rigidly delineated roles within the Church.

But throughout most of history, and still today in many cultures, one's state of life, or caste, has been rigidly fixed. In the United States, where it is quite normal to change jobs, homes, and even careers, the idea of having a fixed state of life is less familiar, especially among the young. Our culture has embraced fluidity to an unhealthy extreme. Moreover, our cultural core is Protestant, with its attendant skepticism toward the Church's "rigid" institutionalized structure and perceived differentiated "classes" of faithful. We see a hint of this in Hans Urs von Balthasar's major work, *The Christian State of Life*.

In this accessible magnum opus, Balthasar takes more than five hundred pages to explain the theological meaning behind states of life. His objective in writing the book was to provide a "comprehensive meditation" on the discernment of that state of life that will most help us achieve our ultimate goal, union with God. Balthasar beautifully articulates the special nature of ordained and consecrated life—which he variously terms the "state of election," "state of perfection," "way of the counsels," and "evangelical state"—in relation to the lay state, which he often refers to as the "way of the commandments."

In later works, focused more on the lay state, Balthasar tempered the degree to which he elevated the priestly and religious states of election over the lay state. The seed of his evolved way of thinking about vocation and states of life can be detected early on in *The Christian State of Life*, when he acknowledges that where one "stands" in the world or in the Church may be viewed as less important than how one responds to God's love:

> From one point of view, the way of the counsels seems unambiguously better than the way of the commandments; from another, the perfection of love seems to be grounded so thoroughly in that disposition of indifference, that is lovingly ready for all that can be asked of it, that it is no longer possible to understand why the way of the counsels should be considered "more perfect" than the way of the commandments. And it is no clearer now ... why the way of love should be split into two paths so fundamentally different that they actually constitute two different "states of

> life." Just as we can conceive of innumerable variations in man's passage from sin to love, so we can conceive here of innumerable calls from God and corresponding Christian vocations that would all issue from the identical point of human readiness. But neither in the naked will of God as such, nor in His loving will can we find any explanation for the existence of these sharply distinguished states of life within the Church.[9]

How and to what degree one's state of life bears upon one's sanctity is a question that has elicited much ink and discussion throughout the history of the Church. It continues to do so to this day. As this question relates to the discussion about the dedicated single vocation, what is pertinent is understanding where a dedicated single person fits into the formal structure of the Church and what differentiates the various states of life. Such an understanding provides helpful clarity for living out one's vocation well. In an effort to identify a place and a role for dedicated singles within the Church, it is useful to understand the historical context and the mind-set of the institutional Church, a task wrought with challenge, given the rapid pace of change inside and outside the Church over the past half century.

The Second Vatican Council documents and Pope St. John Paul II's 1988 apostolic exhortation *Christifideles Laici* (Christ's Faithful People) beautifully articulate the important role of the laity in the Church. By the mid-twentieth century, the pendulum, which had swung too far in the direction of exalting clergy and religious vis-à-vis the laity, was starting to swing back to a more balanced middle ground. The complementarity of the clergy and religious

[9] Hans Urs von Balthasar, *The Christian State of Life*, trans. Sister Mary Frances McCarthy (San Francisco: Ignatius Press, 1983), 57.

and the laity—whether married or single—and of each unique Christian vocation began to gain recognition, thanks, in part, to welcome theological support by these documents.

Singles share this lay state with the married. It has become common in recent years, however, to refer to marriage as its own distinct state, separate from the state of the single life.

The Church's heightened focus on marriage is desperately needed and greatly appreciated. But does referring to marriage as a state of life in the Church diminish the richness of the concept of the general lay state? Does it inadvertently "peripherize" (a Pope Francis verb) single laity, whether transitional, vowed, same-sex attracted, civilly divorced, or widowed?

A vocation is a personal call from God to live out one's life or pursue a particular mission *within* an established state of life. The idea of vocation is more expansive and fluid than the more fixed, structural concept of states of life. God provides the circumstances and the talents to fulfill the vocational mission planned for us. "For we are his handiwork, created in Christ Jesus for the good works that God has prepared in advance, that we should live in them" (Eph. 2:10). He also gives us the freedom to embrace or reject His plans for us.

One may have a number of vocations throughout one's life, or one may have a singular, grand vocation or mission. "God does not give us our vocation as we enter the seminary or enter marriage. We shall find out our vocation at the moment of death," suggests papal theologian Fr. Wojciech Giertych, O.P.[10]

Might we think of St. Jerome's vocation as the translation of Holy Scripture from Greek and Hebrew into Latin? Might St. Joan d'Arc's vocation have been to lead the French in defeat of the English? Was St. Catherine of Siena's vocation to implore

[10] Women's retreat, Stamford, Connecticut, August 2016.

Pope Gregory XI to buck up and return to Rome from his exile in Avignon? As for devout singles who have not been added to the pantheon of recognized saints, might Antoni Gaudí's design of the Basílica de la Sagrada Família in Barcelona, or Jan Tyranowski's spiritual influence on the young Karol Wojtyła (the future Pope John Paul II), or Frank Duff's founding of the Legion of Mary have been their special vocations?

"Vocation" is also understood in the Church to mean a very specific call to the priesthood or to the consecrated life. When we are asked to pray for an increase in vocations at Mass, we all know this is the type of vocation implied. It wasn't until the twentieth century that marriage was widely considered to be a vocation in the Church.

Outside the Church, the term "vocation" refers to a wide array of endeavors, whether it be a particular trade, career, hobby, or parenthood. Given this broader understanding of vocation, one can better appreciate the pushback against those who deny vocational status to singles.

Let's return to St. Francis de Sales's definition of a true vocation: "the firm and constant will possessed by the person called, to want to serve God in the manner and in the place where the Divine Majesty calls her." Again, according to de Sales, a vocation consists of three elements: constancy, a desire to love and serve God, and an embrace of the circumstances in which God calls us. We may add to this definition the element of self-gift, which underpins the Church's understanding of vocation and of general human flourishing.

The single life, when it is transitional, clearly does not correspond to this understanding of a vocational calling in the Church. Singles still discerning God's call or older singles open to marriage, whether or not they peacefully accept God's will for them, are not living out a single vocation.

What constitutes a true single vocation? It is the call to single life as the permanent and providentially ordained means to love and serve God wholeheartedly; the definitive giving of oneself to Christ exclusively and permanently.

As for understanding the deeper underpinnings of the single-vocation question, we can't go wrong with Aquinas. According to the Angelic Doctor, something is perfect "when it attains its proper end." For the human soul, God is its ultimate end. We also know from Scriptures that "God is love, and whoever remains in love remains in God and God in him" (1 John 4:16). Therefore, Aquinas concludes that "the perfection of the Christian life consists principally in charity."[11] We also know from Aquinas that "something is bad when it does not have what is fitting to it, that is, what properly belongs to it." An act is bad when it deviates from one's nature. It leads us away from fulfillment or our ultimate end.[12]

So, in light of Aquinas's teachings, is being single a bad thing, a neutral thing, or a good thing? I think Aquinas would suggest that we still do not have enough information to make a judgment.

Implicitly or explicitly, the single life is viewed by many as bad or, at best, neutral. How many young people aspire to being single all their lives? How many parents pray that their children be single adults? How many priests during Mass ask us to pray for more single vocations? The religious, ordained, and married states are objectively good, irrespective of the sanctity of the individuals who enter these states. In contrast, being single is seen as a neutral and, most often, default state. Understanding its quality or

[11] Thomas Aquinas, *Summa Theologiae*, II-II, q. 184, art. 1.

[12] Stephen J. Heaney, "On Good and Evil in the Things That Afflict Us," *Homiletic and Pastoral Review*, November 6, 2017.

characterizing it depends on external circumstances and internal motives more so than any other state.

Part of the pastoral-outreach challenge for the Church is that, when it comes to singles, generalizations obscure profoundly different personal situations, significantly more so than for religious, ordained, or married states. Single life can entail a wide variety of circumstances, telling us very little of the intent and quality of this way of life. A single person may be living a life of licentious pleasure; willful independence focused on self; holy patience waiting for a spouse or discerning a potential religious call; bitterness for not having found a spouse; or sacrificial resignation over a way of life not chosen. Or the person may be following St. Paul's counsel and living a fully embraced celibate life to love Christ undividedly in the world.

The single life, in itself, does not necessarily go against one's nature or move one away from one's supernatural or even temporal fulfillment. Indeed, being single may lead some more readily to their supernatural end—perfect love of and union with God. But the risks of living as a single person are greater than living in the married or consecrated states. The exterior constraints of marriage and religious life make smoother the road to interior freedom and holiness. How easy it is for exterior freedom, inherent in a single life, to lead to selfishness, a hardening of the heart, and pride of life, the jailers in an interior incarceration. "Whoever loves his life loses it" (John 12:25).

Dietrich von Hildebrand suggests that marriage (and, presumably, religious life) is a powerful antidote to a host of negative traits that can plague singles:

> If the act of marriage when accomplished in the highest way destroys a certain stiff self-containedness [to which singles are susceptible] which tends to harden the heart, blunt the

> susceptibilities, and produce a self-important prig, this peculiar self-containedness is destroyed by marriage with Christ in a far more complete and radical fashion. [13]

In a well-intentioned effort to reach out to the growing number of singles, some in the Church have tried to shift the narrative by characterizing singleness as a blessed good without adequately acknowledging that most have not chosen this way of living out their baptismal vocations.

Others, when making the argument that there is no such thing as a single vocation, seemingly blame singles for having done something wrong, though perhaps unwittingly. The assumption is that singles either did not heed a call to the religious or married states or that they made myriad mistakes in dating, which prevented them from landing a spouse. In the past, however, it was more widely held that someone beyond a certain age without a spouse or a religious habit had rejected a vocation to the consecrated state. The young rich man who walks sadly away from Christ's invitation to the evangelical counsels immediately comes to mind. Surely today there are those who consciously turn away from a clearly discerned vocation to consecrated life.

Not answering a call to religious, ordained, or married life certainly is not good, nor is it simply a neutral act, and it is unhelpful to single souls to whitewash this fact. Balthasar, in *The Christian State of Life*, has strong words to say about the consequences of a rejected call to the "state of election," the consecrated life:

> He causes untold harm who rejects God's call because his "no" affects not only himself, but also all those who depend on his mission. And, in the end, he will be called

[13] Dietrich von Hildebrand, *In Defense of Purity* (Steubenville, OH: Hildebrand Project, 2017), 133.

> to account not only for himself alone, but also for all the graces that have been withheld from the world by reason of his "no".... The greater the mission, the more unique it is. For him who is called to do great things for the Lord, it is a question of all or nothing. If he rejects his mission, he can neither demand nor expect it to be replaced by one that is second-best.[14]

Many of the devout, single Catholic women I know are not single because they rejected a vocation to religious or married life. They are single because the opportunity to marry a virtuous man, to whom it would have been right and fitting to give one's heart, has not presented itself. Others did not discern a call to religious life, despite being truly open to such a call.

Objectively, a rejection of God's design for our lives is a rejection of God's love. But only God can judge our hearts and the import of the circumstances that lead each of us to reject His will for us, whether it be a major vocational call to consecrated life or daily promptings from the Holy Spirit. God typically does not make His calls crystal clear; He is gentler than that, allowing us to wiggle out of His will for us.

The Gospel is full of repentant sinners who, through grace and hard work, turn their lives around and become great disciples of Christ. Might this same dynamic play out for those who grow in love and generosity such that, over time, their wills bend toward God? After all, "we know that all things work for good for those who love God, who are called according to His purpose" (Rom. 8:28).

Take Catherine of Genoa. She felt called to enter the convent as a young teen but was turned away for being too young. She later

[14] Balthasar, *The Christian State of Life*, 498–499.

abided by her parents' wishes and married a nobleman when she was sixteen, rather than holding firm to her earlier calling. Countless saints were coerced, sometimes under pain of death, to marry, but they held firm to their vocational call to virginity or consecrated life. Catherine endured ten years of an awful, abusive marriage, during which she turned to the world for solace. Then, one day, she experienced an intense mystical experience that marked the beginning of the rest of her life, which she spent in service to the poor and the sick in close union with God. Catherine is most known for the profound interior inspirations she experienced, most notably concerning purgatory.

Might St. Catherine of Genoa have effectively rejected her first major vocational call to religious life? God clearly had a major mission for her that, in human terms, would have been better fulfilled as a nun. Instead, provoked by an awful marriage, she strayed for a number of years before God assertively reached out to her to complete a hugely important mission. Was this God's plan all along, or did her less than devoutly lived years "work for good"?

In his typically profound yet gentle manner, Pope Benedict XVI extracts God from the rigid mold we like to create for Him and attributes to His providence much more leeway:

> God did not intend Israel to have a kingdom. The kingdom was a result of Israel's rebellion against God.... God yielded to Israel's obstinacy and so devised a new kind of kingship for them. The King is Jesus; in Him God entered humanity and espoused it to Himself. This is the usual form of the divine activity in relation to mankind. God does not have a fixed plan that He must carry out; on the contrary, He has many different ways of finding man and even of turning his wrong ways into right ways.... The

feast of Christ the King is therefore not a feast of those who are subjugated, but a feast of those who know that they are in the hands of the one who writes straight on crooked lines.[15]

[15] Pope Benedict XVI, as quoted in *Magnificat*, November 26, 2017.

Chapter 3

A Vocation with No Name

He bound Himself so intimately to one woman as to no other on earth: He formed her so closely after His own image as no other human being before or after; He gave her a place in the Church for all eternity such as has been given to no other human being. And just so, He has called women in all times to the most intimate union with Him: they are to be emissaries of His love, proclaimers of His will to kings and popes, and forerunners of His Kingdom in the hearts of men. To be the Spouse of Christ is the most sublime vocation which has been given, and whoever sees this way open before her will yearn for no other way.[16]

A roadblock to a broader understanding of the dedicated single vocation within the lay state is the fact that being single in generic terms tells us very little. "Single" encompasses a wide diversity of motives and lived expressions, from celibacy to libertine licentiousness, and everything in between. This contrasts with married, ordained, and religious life, in which the lived norms are widely known and embraced, even by those who fail to meet the respective "requirements."

I think the question of terminology is more important than it may seem at first blush. How helpful it would be for us who are

[16] Edith Stein, "Vocations of Man and Woman," in *Essays on Woman* (Washington, D.C.: ICS Publications, 1996), 94.

called to permanent single life for the express purpose of glorifying God to be able to express our vocation in widely understood terms. This would bring others to understand and perhaps appreciate our special vocation as one distinct from most singles—who are in a transitional phase of life, discerning or waiting for their vocation (to marriage) to be realized—and, of course, distinct from those living outside the norms prescribed by God and the Church.

Confusion and lack of precision in vocabulary concerning single Catholics abound. Owing to time I've spent with Dominicans, I think it useful to attempt some definitional clarity on the matter.

The word "chaste" comes from the Latin *castus*, meaning "clean" or "morally pure." It is the moral virtue of handling one's sexuality properly and in accord with one's state of life. For a single person, chastity means not engaging in sexual relations, whereas married couples can be both chaste and have sexual relations. Singles and religious, however, can abstain from sex and still be unchaste by letting unchaste desires in their minds run amok or by viewing pornography.

All baptized men and women are called to live chastely. Indeed, "a life project that ultimately is to be based upon charity requires such an integration of sexuality that manifests respect for the human dignity and corporal and spiritual finality of the self and of the other."[17] The anti-procreative, contraceptive mind-set pervading today's culture encourages a distorted understanding of the true good of self and others, as well as the true meaning of sexuality. This makes the exercise of chastity more difficult, even

[17] Wojciech Giertych, O.P., "The Virtue of Chastity in Marriage: Its Reality and Difficulties," *Doctor Communis* Annuario/2 della Pontificia Accademia di San Tommaso d'Aquino: *San Tommaso il matrimonio e la famiglia* a cura di Serge-Thomas Bonino e Guido Mazzota (Città del Vaticano: Urbaniania University Press, 2019), 219–236.

for those who are living out consecrated chastity, according to Fr. Wojciech Giertych. The sexual scandal in our Church today and the turn-a-blind-eye response by Church hierarchy have made this painfully clear.

According to Aquinas, the cardinal virtue temperance (which chastity is intimately tied to) helps to manage properly the power of our emotions or passions. Chastity can be acquired as a natural virtue, being a manifestation of temperance, or it can develop as a supernatural virtue rooted in charity, the fruit of grace, brought about through prayer. Sometimes it is entirely appropriate for the passions to express themselves, such as in artistic endeavors, and depending on temperament, one may be more or less passionate, requiring a greater or lesser exercising of temperance. So, for highly passionate rock stars constantly exposed to occasions of sin, virtue formation through prayer and effort is especially important. One should not wonder why there are so few chaste rock stars.

"Perfect chastity" means no sexual relations for one's entire life, and it is often used interchangeably with "celibacy." Celibacy, however, is the state of voluntarily choosing to be unmarried, so it is not exactly the same as simply being single. Celibacy has deep historical roots and various lived expressions. The Church distinguishes between lay and ecclesiastical celibacy, though in both cases the person freely chooses, for religious reasons, to remain celibate.

Continence, on the other hand, is the active choice not to engage in sexual relations. It comes from the Latin word *continentia*, meaning holding back.[18] Priests, religious, and all faithful singles

[18] Fr. Giertych explains the important distinction Aquinas makes between chastity and continence: "Aquinas distinguishes between *castitas* and *continentia*. Chastity is a moral virtue allied with temperance. It is located within the sexual desire itself that adapts to the true good of the other. The virtue is within the sensitive

are called to practice continence in particular ways, as with chastity. Even married couples may choose continence under certain circumstances. Married Eastern-rite priests are expected to practice continence before they celebrate Mass and during other religious feasts so that they can be singularly focused on God.

In a world that glorifies, fetishizes, and even worships sex, is it any surprise that chastity, continence, and celibacy have taken on negative connotations?

Some terms for the vocational single life that I've heard or have come up with myself are as follows: lay single, lay celibate, vowed single, vowed lay single, dedicated single, dedicated lay single, committed single, chaste single, vowed celibate, lay celibate, non-vowed single,[19] apostolic single, consecrated lay—a carload of descriptive names with similar, though not identical, meanings.

---

movement, the emotion, that has an intrinsic need to follow the rational mean—*appetitus sensitivus natus est obedire rationi*. Chastity tempers not the sexual pleasure itself, which may be limitless, but the attachment to the pleasure. *Continentia* is located not in the emotion, but in the will, which stops short the movement of the passion. As such, it is not really a virtue. It is an emergency reaction of the one who is not yet virtuous, but who blocks the sexual emotion by sheer will-power. The virtuous do the right thing easily, speedily, with pleasure, and creatively. The continent stop short, as if through a sudden pressing on the brake. This does not bring interior peace, but prevents one from engaging in disordered action. All this has to be also distinguished from a neurotic attempt to block the emotions, by some other emotion, such as fear or emotional energy. These distinctions are found in Aquinas. In common parlance, these words, of course, are not so precise."

[19] Patricia A. Sullivan, "The Nonvowed Form of the Lay State in the Life of the Church," *Theological Studies* 68 (June 2007). This was one of the few articles I came across that theologically addresses the question of vocation and single lay Catholics. I found it to be very helpful, and I am grateful to its author.

I have heard the term "chaste single" used to describe the vocational single life. But we do not normally qualify those living in the married state as "chaste married" (even though chastity is necessary in marriage) or priests as "chaste ordained," as much as we hope they *are* chaste. All of us are called to be chaste, so why refer to this vocation broadly as "chaste single"? We might refer to someone as a chaste single when emphasizing the virtue of chastity in that person. And we may have come to the point in today's sexualized culture where "chaste" is an important distinguishing modifier for any single. The term, however, doesn't provide enough specificity to be used generally for those who discern a vocation as a single layperson, in my opinion.

"Lay celibate" is the most technically precise term, as it conveys the idea of an actively chosen, permanent commitment to this vocational call. It also clearly expresses the notion that this vocation entails a directing of one's primary affections to God while living in the secular world, rather than in a religious community or as an ordained priest. But *should* single laypersons, who discern a call to bind themselves to Christ exclusively, refer to themselves as "lay celibate"? Should we reclaim the word "celibate," which has taken on a negative connotation, and wear it proudly?[20] Generally speaking, I think not, because it risks feeding the gravely mistaken sex-as-identity, reductionist mind-set pervasive today. We are so much more than a narrowly circumscribed identity classification, whether it be according to skin color, ethnicity, or sexual orientation. Using narrowly defined identity profiles misses the essential core of who we are—wonderfully complex children of a loving Father. This implies a unity infinitely more important than our differences might suggest.

[20] The derogatory term "queer" was reclaimed and turned into a badge of honor.

Proudly proclaiming a celibate label could serve as an effective, mind-bending counterpunch to sexual or gender identity labels and their narrow, often soul-killing ultimate aims. The use of "celibate," however, would probably serve to replace one anthropologically flawed label with another, as edifying as the new label may be. Celibacy is not the core of either the religious vocation or the dedicated single vocation. Embracing celibacy is a *consequence* of choosing Christ as our all. Celibacy is not the primary motive or defining characteristic.

Moreover, the term may put an unnecessary stumbling block in front of those who may be curious about this vocation. The idea of celibacy is so foreign to many that it may be nearly impossible to contemplate. Celibacy is difficult to understand in today's culture. Many can fathom on some level a religious or priest being celibate but not a "normal," attractive single person living fully in the world, choosing a life with God as its apex over a slew of other things.

Interestingly, however, celibacy should not be so difficult to envision for certain secular people. Many of us know of diehard athletes, entrepreneurs, scientists, or writers who forsake much, including sex, for a greater goal. Our culture has become more sexualized overall, yet, for some high achievers, sex is being displaced by intense activities in other realms.

Through the writing of this book, I've come to prefer the term "dedicated single" vocation. "Dedicated" originates from the Latin *dedicare*, meaning "devoted" or "consecrated," thus conveying the notions of permanence and the embracing of a greater good. "Single" is obvious. Where variety or grammar calls for it, I use the term "lay celibacy" throughout this book in addition to "dedicated single," though I generally do not use this expression in conversation.

I think "committed single" works well too. "Committed" originates from the Latin *committare*, meaning "to join" or "to entrust."

But to me, "committed" feels more clinical, less richly textured than "dedicated."

Why not include "lay" in the description? Indeed, the fact that this vocation is lived out within the lay state is a critically important element in this way of life, clearly distinguishable from the religious state. A risk for dedicated singles is to attempt to live as religious wannabes, but this is not our calling. Having said this, I think "single" makes it quite clear that this is a lay, not a religious, vocation. I've never heard a nun referred to as single, and the only time I've heard the word "single" in reference to the priestly vocation was in a talk given about the "Hidden Christians" of Japan.[21]

Why not call a single person, unaffiliated with a secular institute, a "consecrated layperson"? Actually, *all* baptized Christians are consecrated. "Consecrated" originates from the Latin *consecrare*, meaning "made holy," "sacred," "set apart," "dedicated to God." Baptism is the momentous event of our lives when God brings us into His fold. And our response should be to dedicate ourselves to God: "I urge you therefore, brothers, by the mercies of God, to offer your bodies as a living sacrifice, holy and pleasing to God" (Rom. 12:1).

[21] According to the talk "Hidden Christians in Japan: The History of an Oriental Miracle," by Japanese Jesuit Shinzo Kawamura, professor of Church history at Sophia University in Tokyo, delivered on October 12, 2017, at the Gregorian University in Rome, around the year 1700, during the persecution of Christians in Japan, a faithful catechist and martyr named Bastian predicted that priests would return to the island some 250 years later to administer the sacraments again. To determine whether those future confessors were really Catholic priests, Bastian told the members of the Christian community to ask them the following three questions: "Are you single? What is the name of your leader in Rome? Do you venerate the Blessed Virgin Mary?"

The term "consecrated" has come to mean something very specific in Church parlance. According to canon law, "consecrated" refers explicitly to those who have made permanent vows either in a canonically recognized religious order or institute, or directly to a bishop, as consecrated virgins do. Normally, the vows are the three evangelical counsels of poverty, chastity, and obedience, and they are professed publicly. Members of secular institutes are consecrated, but they retain the lay state. Whereas religious touch the world with the richness of their consecrated lives from *without*, being present to the world from their monasteries and convents, consecrated members of secular institutes touch the world with the richness of their consecrated lives *within* the world but in a more hidden fashion than that of habited religious. Dedicated singles, who make private promises or vows to God, also touch the world from within, in an even more hidden way. They are more on their own than members of secular institutes, who generally participate in a common formation program, as do religious.

The Rise of Singles

Fewer people are getting married. This relatively recent and growing phenomenon has major social implications that are only beginning to be appreciated.

In 1946, 2.3 million couples wed and another 610,000 divorced. This first post–WW II year witnessed the peak marriage rate in U.S. history — 16 marriages per 1,000 people. In 2010, there were only 7 marriages per 1,000 people, and this rate has continued to decline.[22]

[22] Centers for Disease Control–National Center for Health Statistics data configured in a chart by Randy Olsen, referenced in Ana Swanson, "144 Years of Marriage and Divorce in the United States, in One Chart," *Washington Post*, June 23, 2015.

Looked at another way, in 1965, only 17 percent of adults between the ages of 21 and 36 had never been married, according to Pew Research. By 2017, the percentage of never-married adults had jumped to 57 percent of the population! For young adults under the age of 30, the likelihood of being married is slim—about 20 percent today, versus nearly 60 percent who were married by the age of 30 in 1960. And since 2009, unmarried women have outnumbered married women for the first time ever.

Economic Explanation

Viewed through a purely economic lens, the blame for declining marriage rates is placed on the shoulders of men who are falling behind professionally. Millennial men remain less likely to hold down a job than the generation before them, while women their age are working at higher rates.

Though employment rates fully recovered from the Great Recession of 2008–2009, young men have not caught up: 25- to 34-year-old men lag in the workforce more than any other age and gender demographic. For these prime-age males, the employment (participation) rate remains at depressed levels—86 percent, compared with 91 percent recorded before the 2008 financial crisis. For men with a high school diploma or less, the participation rate is even worse—currently at 83 percent, down from 97 percent recorded in 1964. About 500,000 more young, marriage-age men would be working today had the employment rate returned to pre-downturn levels.[23]

Unemployment will continue to have profoundly negative effects, not only on these nonworking men but on our entire society. Most directly, this phenomenon hurts their marriage-age female counterparts.

[23] Jeanna Smialek, "Millennial Men Leave Perplexing Hole in Hot U.S. Job Market," Bloomberg, November 2, 2018.

What is the reason for this grim male-employment situation? A much-discussed explanation is outsourcing and automation. Technological change has exacerbated the male unemployment problem through new, labor-replacing technologies. The trend shows no sign of decelerating, and, if it continues, a third of working-age men will not be working by the mid-twenty-first century. According to the management consulting firm McKinsey and Company, under a "midpoint" scenario, some 39 million American jobs, the majority held by men, will be displaced by automation by 2030.[24] Another strategic management consulting firm, Bain and Company, forecasts that the new automation wave could displace 2.5 million workers a year, impacting more men than women. This compares with the 1.2 million people a year displaced in the agricultural upheaval from 1900 to 1940, after adjusting for population, and the 800,000 a year in the onset of the information age from 1970 to 1990.[25]

Chinese factories are even blamed for the reducing male employment and, hence, marriage rates. A recent study claims that increased trade with China has reduced marriage rates in the U.S. by approximately 1 percent in recent years.[26]

Other social changes could also be exacerbating the lower male-employment trend. High-quality video games and online activity makes leisure time more attractive. Opioid use makes men less employable. The reduced stigma of young adults living at home and cohabitating reduces the incentive to earn a paycheck.

[24] McKinsey and Company, "Jobs Lost, Jobs Gained: Workforce Transitions in a Time of Automation," 2017.

[25] Karen Harris, "A Long Disruption Is Ahead with Low-Paying Jobs," Macro Trends Group, Bain and Company, April 4, 2018.

[26] David Autor, David Dorn, Gordon Hansen, "When Work Disappears: Manufacturing Decline and the Failing Marriage-Market Value of Men," NBER Working Paper 23173, February 2017.

Disaggregating the data by socioeconomic class reveals that poorer, less-educated Americans marry at rates much lower than those who are wealthier and more educated. But they still have children. Single parenthood is highly correlated with poverty, underemployment and unemployment, and high incarceration rates.[27]

As a growing number of men flounder economically, more women are thriving. The fastest job growth in recent decades has been in traditionally feminine "pink collar" sectors, called HEAL jobs—health, education, administration, and literacy. Young women today are the first in modern history to start their work lives being paid at rates nearly equal with those of men, with hourly wages for young-adult females at 93 percent of that of men. College-educated women who do not marry until their thirties earn $18,000 more per year than equivalently educated women who marry in their twenties.[28] The lack of marriage and its responsibilities has enabled women to advance faster and higher than their younger, married counterparts, on average. In contrast, college-educated men earn more money when they marry early.

Political Explanation

Viewed from a traditional or more conservative political lens, the declining rate of marriage is the fault of women. As the argument goes, women have ruptured millennia of social norms and weakened the family for selfish pursuits and ersatz independence.

Leftists laud this radical social upheaval, representing in their minds women's long-hoped-for emancipation from the patriarchal

[27] This sociological phenomenon was powerfully exposed in Charles Murray's book *Coming Apart: The State of White America, 1960–2010*.

[28] Kay Hymowitz, Jason S. Carroll, W. Bradford Wilcox, and Kelleen Kaye, "Knot Yet Report: The Benefits and Costs of Delayed Marriage in America," 2003.

and rigid social norms that unjustly forced them into marriage. Rebecca Traister, in her 2016 book *All the Single Ladies: Unmarried Women and the Rise of an Independent Nation*, makes exactly this case:

> It is a radical upheaval, a national reckoning with massive social and political implications. Across classes, and races, we are seeing a wholesale revision of what female life might entail. We are living through the invention of independent female adulthood as a norm, not an aberration, and the creation of an entirely new population: adult women who are no longer economically, socially, sexually, or reproductively dependent on or defined by the men they marry.... The rise of the single woman is an exciting turn of historical events because it entails a complete rethinking of who women are and what family is and who holds dominion within it—and outside it.
>
> Beyond whether you regard this shift as dangerous or thrilling, it is having a profound effect on our politics. While they are not often credited for it, single women's changed circumstances are what's driving a political agenda that seems to become more progressive every day[29].

Sexual Promiscuity Explanation

In *Cheap Sex: The Transformation of Men, Marriage and Monogamy*, Mark Regneris lays out in depressing detail the case for how moral decline, particularly sexual promiscuity, has depressed marriage rates. Regneris spends 260 pages hammering home the real-world

[29] Rebecca Traister, *All the Single Ladies: Unmarried Women and the Rise of an Independent Nation* (New York, Simon and Schuster, 2016), quoted in Rebecca Traister, "Single Women Are Now the Most Potent Political Force in America," *New York Magazine*, February 22, 2016.

ramifications of the expression "Why buy a cow when you can get the milk for free?"

> Nowadays young men can skip the wearying detour of getting education and career prospects to qualify for sex. Nor does he have to get married and accept all those costs, including promising to share his lifetime earnings and forgo other women forever. Female sex partners are available without all that.... Sex has become free and easy. This is today's version of the opiate of the (male) masses.[30]

That our culture has become hypersexualized is acknowledged by most of us. What may not be fully appreciated is just how egregious it is. An often-repeated refrain from young, devout Catholic women I know is that guys lose interest in them when they find out that premarital sex is off the table. Even some of my nonreligious friends have become alarmed, now that their daughters have entered their teenage years. Their daughters provide firsthand reports about the hookup culture predominating on most university and high school campuses. I was a bit amused by the suggestion that a nonchurchgoing friend of mine gave her daughter: "Seek out the religious guys on campus, as they are less likely to engage in the hookup scene."

During the fiftieth-anniversary year of the publication of *Humanae Vitae*, a number of commentaries highlighted the negative impact the wholesale rejection of the encyclical and the widespread use of birth control has had on society. The explosion of "safe sex" has deformed people, especially men, who are wounded differently than women. Men are wounded in their identity because they do not grow in paternal virtues, and, in fact, any potential child

[30] Quoted in Mark Regneris, *Cheap Sex* (New York: Oxford University Press, 2017), 149.

that may result from sex becomes the enemy. When procreation is excluded from sex, it generates egoism. What remains is like a drug, and what a drug sex has become!

The U.S. porn industry, which represents about 10 percent of the global porn market, generates an estimated $10 to $12 billion-plus in revenue annually. According to Juniper Research, some 136 billion adult videos were watched in 2015, and they expect this figure to skyrocket to 193 billion by 2020. Globally, each smartphone user of adult content is expected to watch an average of 348 videos this year, with the biggest growth expected to occur in the U.S., where video views are predicted to grow by over 50 percent by 2020. According to a 2014 survey, 64 percent of American men view porn at least monthly. And if you think this rate is lower for Christian men, you are sadly mistaken.[31]

Add to this the rapidly growing "mature videogame" market, targeting primarily men. It exceeds $100 billion in annual revenues globally. Nintendo recently released an adult videogame called "Gal*Gun2*," in which gamers shoot pheromone shots to agitate screens full of young girls. Let us not imagine the raucous, idea-generating sessions led by adolescent-minded Internet coders who developed this nonedifying concept. The computer screen has become the focal point of too many unemployed marriage-age men.

In his pastoral yet profound way, Archbishop Chaput summarized the impact of the current moral morass:

> The truth about our sexuality is that infidelity, promiscuity, sexual confusion, and mass pornography create human wreckage. Multiply that wreckage by tens of millions of persons over five decades. Then compound it with media

[31] "Pornography Use and Addiction," quoted in Judy Keane, *Single and Catholic* (Manchester, NH: Sophia Institute Press, 2016), 82.

> nonsense about the innocence of casual sex and the "happy" children of friendly divorces. What you get is what we have now: a dysfunctional culture of frustrated and wounded people increasingly incapable of permanent commitments, self-sacrifice, and sustained intimacy, and unwilling to face the reality of their own problems. Weak and selfish individuals make weak and selfish marriages. Weak and selfish marriages make broken families. And broken families continue and spread the cycle of dysfunction. They do it by creating more and more wounded individuals. [32]

Selfish Unwillingness to Commit

Some choose not to marry out of selfish motives. In my experience, this critique is levied more by those who practice their faith seriously than by those with no religious affiliation. The following quotation from a young woman might understandably crystalize the singles-are-selfish thesis:

> I know it sounds hyperbolic, but I mean it when I say that getting married right now would ruin my life. I want freedom. I want the chance to pick up and move to a new city for a new job or for adventure, without having to worry about a spouse or family. I need to be able to stay at the office until three in the morning if I have to and not care about putting dinner on the table.[33]

Pope Francis spoke specifically to this woman's mind-set in *Amoris Laetitia*:

[32] Charles J. Chaput, O.F.M. Cap., 2016 Tocqueville Lecture, University of Notre Dame, September 15, 2016.

[33] A senior at Northwestern University interviewed by Rebecca Traister, quoted in Traister, "Single Women."

> The ideal of marriage, marked by a commitment to exclusivity and stability, is swept aside whenever it proves inconvenient or tiresome. The fear of loneliness and the desire for stability and fidelity exist side by side with a growing fear of entrapment in a relationship that could hamper the achievement of one's personal goals.[34]

Undoubtedly, a selfish desire for radical autonomy plays a role in the rise of singles today. But, in my experience, the number of women who earnestly desire to get married or who discern a call to lay celibacy vastly exceeds the number of those who choose not to marry due to a yearning for independence. Moreover, the reality on the ground typically does not break into an all-selfish versus all-giving dichotomy.

Yes, there are more than a few who still want it all, meaning they want great careers that require long hours and travel, in addition to great marriages and thriving children. One need only read the vicious responses to Anne-Marie Slaughter's 2012 *Atlantic* article "Why Women Still Can't Have It All" to see that this mind-set persists, particularly amongst college graduates who entered the workforce in the 1970s, '80s and '90s.

But is the other extreme any better? Quoting Rebecca Traister again:

> By the end of the 1950s, around 60 percent of female students were dropping out of college, either to marry or because the media blitz and realignment of expectations led them to believe that further education would inhibit their chances of finding a husband. In his 1957 *Harper's* piece "American

[34] Pope Francis, Post-Synodal Apostolic Exhortion *Amoris Laetitia* (March 19, 2016), no. 3.

> Youth Goes Monogamous," Charles Cole, president of Amherst College, wrote that "a girl who gets as far as her junior year in college without having acquired a man is thought to be in grave danger of becoming an old maid." In these years, around half of brides were younger than 20, and 14 million women were engaged by the time they were 17.[35]

Work-family balance and the respective roles of men and women in the family are delicate, highly charged, important topics beyond the scope of this book. One observation I'll make is that I cannot recall having felt judged for being single or for being "selfishly" career-focused in any of the secular environments in which I have operated. Moreover, my parents never pushed me toward marriage.

The one and only comment I remember being made by a family member about my single status was at my grandmother's funeral. My father and I were waiting at the back of the church to walk together to our designated seats in the front. Before proceeding, my father turned to me and quipped, "I guess this will be the only chance I get to walk you down the aisle." My mental response: "Where the heck did that come from?"—as it was so out of character for my father. And I was young, I thought, only thirty-three years old. It is only recently that I have come to appreciate how fortunate I was that my parents neither pressured me, nor judged me (as far as I know) for not getting married.

A close friend of mine often recounts the wise words her father gave her when she asked him for advice about a man she was dating. This saintly man of few words advised, "Better to be a little lonely than to spend one's life in Hell." In contrast, I have seen countless women pressured to marry at all costs. Often these women are made to feel less worthy without a wedding ring. If only parents,

[35] Traister, "Single Women."

even those acting out of goodwill, knew how unhelpful and even wounding the pressure to marry can be for those who take their faith seriously and who either desire to get married or who do not do so for edifying reasons!

At what point does developing one's God-given gifts outside of marriage and childbearing shift from being lauded stewardship in support of the common good to being self-aggrandizement? The unsettling choice of words aside, should we completely discount the perspective of the Northwestern University senior quoted above? Is there no merit in finishing university and then spending a few years focused on developing one's temporal gifts in society? Does the desire to explore and figure out one's place in the world contradict the desire to get married, even later in one's thirties? Should a woman who discerns a vocation to marriage make this her number-one priority during her university years and right afterward, even to the exclusion of activities that would develop other talents?

Here is where I sometimes see a disconnect between the generations, made crystal clear in a conversation I had with the father of a student of mine. When I commented that his daughter is a hard-working, motivated student with an enthusiastic interest in pursuing a business career, he expressed heartfelt concern for her future since, at the age of twenty-seven, she exhibited no interest in marriage. When I suggested that perhaps she may not be called to marriage, he insisted that he envisioned his daughter not as a highly successful businesswoman but as the *wife* of a businessman. Changing tactics, I suggested that, due to the wounded nature of so many young men today, many in the grips of pornography addiction, it may be that she will not meet a man capable of entering into a sacramental marriage. He countered that women need to sacrifice because, after all, marriage is a sacrifice.

Is his daughter being selfish by not potentially marrying (and, presumably, redeeming) a pornography-addicted or unemployed man? Will she come to regret her exuberant focus on a business career if she is still single at forty?

Spiritually speaking, every age has its particular strengths and weaknesses. Sixteenth-century Spaniards were full of holy zeal and ardor, attributes that were critical to their successful, centuries-long fight reclaiming their country from the Moors and to their missionary outreach to Latin America. On the downside, overzealous ardor against intellectual heresy or for the sake of evangelization in Latin America trampled on the rights of more than a few. And a proclivity toward extreme physical mortifications to reign in sensual appetites sometimes veered into self-inflicted violence.

What a profoundly different age we live in, spiritually speaking. The spiritual weakness of developed societies today is tepidity or lack of faith, a corrupted view of freedom, and a restless seeking of sensual pleasures, which have drained our moral energies. How beautifully ironic that it may be chaste singles, both transitional and dedicated—full of ardor and holy zeal—who represent a powerful leavening force amid the spiritual malaise of our age.

Chapter 4

Rehabilitating Celibacy

In the eyes of some non-Catholics, the "Holy Trinity" comprises the pope, the Virgin Mary, and celibacy. Pope Francis has "redeemed" the role of supreme pontiff for many skeptics, and, when it comes down to it, few people view the Blessed Mother with hostility. This is not the case with celibacy. Whereas non-Catholics in ages past generally admired celibates, or at least viewed celibacy as some unattainable practice, many today, including some Catholics, seem to dismiss the notion of celibacy, if they are not threatened by it. To these people, I would recommend reading Isaiah 5:20: "Woe to those who call evil good, and good evil" (RSVCE).

Celibacy and the role it plays in the unfolding of God's plan has its roots in the Old Testament. But it was Jesus Christ, the Virgin Mary, and, ultimately, the twelve apostles who put celibacy on the proverbial map. Celibacy, along with poverty and obedience, make up three of the most important evangelical counsels that came to constitute a distinct and highly valued state of life in the Church.[36]

The evangelical counsels are means to follow Jesus' personal way of life more literally. They help one to follow God's commandments—which we are *all* expected to follow—and to grow in

[36] Other evangelical counsels include: turn the other cheek, forgive seven times seven times, take up your cross, and feed the poor.

virtue. Objectively living out the counsels, however, is not obligatory for all Christians; indeed, of the three counsels, only celibacy can be followed most readily in both the lay and religious states. But it does behoove all Christians to follow the *spirit* of the three counsels. That is to say, we should tame overzealous shopping habits and should follow the Holy Spirit's promptings and obey worldly authorities. And *all* of us are called to chastity.

Historical Backdrop

Celibacy for the Kingdom has traditionally been deemed the "more perfect state," in large part because this is how Christ and our Blessed Mother lived. There is no end to the beautiful, celibacy-extoling prose written throughout the history of the Church.

The way Christians express their baptismal vocations in the concrete circumstances of their daily lives has varied over the Catholic Church's two millennia. Living an authentically Christian life during the early days of the Church meant being a courageous witness to a persecuted Faith, and it could mean martyrdom. From the earliest days of Christianity, deeply faithful women embraced virginity in imitation of Christ and our Blessed Mother, living primarily with their families.[37] There is a reason why, in the Mass's Eucharistic Prayer I, a number of early Church virgins—Felicity, Perpetua, Agatha, Lucy, Agnes, Cecilia, Anastasia—are given prominence of place, reflective of the great honor and respect the

[37] The January 17, 2019, Office of Readings includes a letter by St. Athanasius (296–373) that speaks about the life of St. Antony of the Desert (251–356). In this letter, Athanasius mentions how Antony "placed his sister in the care of some well-known and trustworthy virgins and arranged for her to be brought up in the convent." So, as early as the third century, the notion of "convent" was used to express the communal living of female virgins or celibates.

Church has for these young women two thousand years after their heroic deaths.

It wasn't until the persecution of Christians abated at the end of the third century, after Emperor Constantine's embrace of Christianity, that asceticism, the precursor to the monastic movement and subsequent religious orders, emerged as a distinctive force within the Church.

Once Christianity became widely accepted and Christians blended more readily into society, it became all too easy to embrace the mores of the broader environment. Accordingly, being a witness to the Faith started to require some form of separation from the rest of society:

> The persecution made less solitaries [celibates] than did the peace and triumph of the Church. The Christians, simple and opposed to any softness, were more fearful of a peace that might be gratifying to the senses than they had been of the cruelty of the tyrants.[38]

Many Christians went off to the desert in search of a more "hard-core" religious experience. In the Egyptian desert we find the roots of the religious life. Eventually, the life of the evangelical counsels found their place northward, in the formally structured religious communities of the Middle Ages, playing a prominent role in nearly all facets of European society and culture.

The age we live in increasingly resembles the early years of Christian persecution, and, arguably, things may get worse. Pre-Christian societies, which did not know Christ, were attracted

[38] François Fénelon, "Discours sur les avantages et les devoirs de la vie religieuse," in *Oeuvres* 17, p. 396, quoted in Jordan Aumann, *Christian Spirituality in the Catholic Tradition* (San Francisco: Ignatius Press, 1985), 35.

to the early Christians and were open to a new Christian order. Post-Christian societies have *rejected* Christ, pushing aside love from the public square. Accordingly, does it not follow that this age requires a more radical, heroic Christian witness? For a secular society unmoored from its Christian roots, might there be a need for more Christian witnesses to live embedded, even hidden, within society? How precious is the love of God, flowing from Christ's dedicated and often anonymous emissaries in today's harsh, deracinated landscapes.

Celibacy Today

Celibacy gets little respect these days. Worse, it is widely viewed as therapy inducing, a bit nutty, or positively medieval. Given our sex-obsessed culture, it's no wonder celibacy gets such bad press.

It is hard to imagine that, in the past, celibates were warned about the sin of pride, owing to the fact that celibacy was held in such high esteem. St. Augustine wrote:

> The more clearly I see the greatness of this gift, the more truly do I fear lest it be plundered by thieving pride. No one therefore protects virginity, but God Himself Who bestowed it: and "God is charity." The guardian therefore of virginity is charity; the habitat of this guardian is humility.[39]

Because of the world's contempt for chastity, many celibates today assume the double mantle of celibacy and humility. What a contrast with times past.

Our culture is imbued with the mistaken Gnostic notion that the mental or spiritual self is the true core of the person, with sex having little significance beyond the emotional level and our bodies being little more than something to be manipulated to serve our

[39] *Sacra Virginitas*, no. 60.

"true" selves. Technology and medical advancements have fed this idea that biology need not be a determinant of one's "true" self. We are witnessing no less than a metaphysical revolution. It's no wonder that celibacy makes little sense in this environment. Rejecting the notion that the physical body we were born with is an integral part of what it means to be human necessarily deprecates the value of celibacy. If we are not unified beings, with body and soul playing critical, intertwined roles, celibacy is rendered futile; giving up sex is little more fruitful than giving up chocolate.

Because of the broadly held, mistaken notion that religious practice is primarily associated with an obligation to follow rules, celibacy has come to be viewed as an unrealistic, anachronistic mortification done to appease an exacting God. In the past, when hierarchy was respected and obedience was embraced as a positive virtue, celibacy was viewed with respect. But a rules-based religion, no longer supported by the scaffolding of obedience and institutional legitimacy, has a hard time making the case for celibacy, especially in a rebellious, sexualized wider culture.

Making the case for celibacy is even more difficult when clergy seek affirmation, rather than accept the bitter fruit of speaking hard truths or when, deep down, many in the Church really don't believe in its value:

> When the Church herself doesn't value celibacy at its true value, it is all but impossible to recommend celibacy to others. The less robust and exemplary the celibate example in the Church, the more the idea spreads that the choice for God costs nothing. The less celibacy is apprehended and lived as a grace, the more it begins to be thought of as a punishment.[40]

[40] Patricia Snow, "Dismantling the Cross," *First Things* (April 2015).

Marriage Has Dethroned Celibacy

From its very foundation, celibacy for the Kingdom has held a special place of honor in the Church and has been referred to as the "state of perfection." Celibacy consecrated to God gives birth to the life of the counsels, more commonly known as religious life. This doesn't mean that celibates are necessarily holier than married persons. Rather, celibacy for the Kingdom provides special advantages—a way of life that enables one to be singularly focused on God.

And this doesn't mean that celibates are any worthier than married persons. Rather, differentiated election means that God has chosen some to be blessed in a unique way, so as to serve as conduits of His grace for others, just as God chose the Jews to play a unique role in salvation history.

This thinking goes against today's heightened focus on equality, particularly in the West. The idea that God does not distribute graces equally or that God calls some to a "more perfect" state of life is anathema to our equality-obsessed mind-set. Interestingly, though, in my experience, laity seem to appreciate the special vocation of ordained priesthood and religious life more than some priests and religious do. It seems to me that radical egalitarianism, rooted in the thought of Martin Luther, has been embraced by some in the Church.

As the number of singles has increased precipitously in recent decades, public discourse has increasingly emphasized marriage. The heightened focus on marriage is a critically needed response to the breakdown of marriage and family that has caused so much damage to our society.

But might there also be a downside to a heightened focus on marriage? Has marriage become idolized? Is marriage "essential" for our happiness, as Supreme Court Justice Anthony Kennedy writes?

> Rising from the most basic human needs, marriage is essential to our most profound hopes and aspirations.... Their [homosexuals'] hope is not to be condemned to live in loneliness, excluded from one of civilization's oldest institutions.[41]

Has the Church also embraced the marriage-equals-happiness mind-set? Parts of *Amoris Laetitia* seem materially equivalent to Justice Kennedy's understanding of marriage (and sex) as an essential ingredient in happiness.

One of the encyclical's infamous notes states that continence practiced by couples who are living in second unions after a sacramental marriage may imperil a couple's faith and cause their children to suffer:

> In such situations [divorce and civil remarriage], many people, knowing and accepting the possibility of living "as brothers and sisters" which the Church offers them, point out that if certain expressions of intimacy are lacking, "it often happens that faithfulness is endangered and the good of the children suffers." (329)

As supporting evidence, the note cites paragraph 51 in *Gaudium et Spes*, which refers to the dangers of continence practiced by sacramentally married couples seeking to manage family size, *not* couples in second, civil-union marriages.

The point here is that celibacy has become devalued partly because marriage and sex are held up as a condition for happiness and even of faithfulness, as note 329 in *Amoris Laetitia* seems to imply.[42]

[41] Supreme Court Justice Anthony Kennedy, statement given in *Obergefell v. Hodges*.

[42] Given this condition for happiness, how can marriage or sex be denied to the divorced or to those with same-sex attractions? Even

Pressing this point further, continence has been deemed too hard for the average Christian. A stark light was cast on this normally unspoken thinking by Cardinal Kasper in a remark made ahead of the 2015–2016 synod on the family:

> To live together as brother and sister? Of course I have high respect for those who are doing this. But it's a heroic act, and heroism is not for the average Christian. That could also create new tensions.[43]

This speaks for itself.

One of my favorite films, *Ida*, is about a Polish postulant, Anna, in Communist Poland in the early 1960s. The wise mother superior tells Anna, who had been taken in by the nuns as an orphaned baby, that, before professing her final vows, she should take a leave from the convent to spend time with her aunt in the secular world. Her aunt, a dissolute, agnostic, highly placed Communist functionary, bluntly informs Anna that she is Jewish and that the name given to her at birth was Ida. Anna/Ida accepts this with equanimity and eventually falls in love with an exciting, sensitive, handsome man who clearly loves her in return. In response to Anna/Ida's question to him about what their future together would look like, he lists the daily activities they would do together as a married couple. She repeatedly asks, "Is that all?"

In the next and final scene of the movie (spoiler alert), we see Anna/Ida dressed again in her postulant habit, walking resolutely

after acknowledging the theologically nuanced differences between the severity of the sins of premarital and homosexual sex, I understand why the fact that priests and laity turn a blind eye to the former while holding firm against the latter is a bitter pill for some to swallow.

43 Matthew Boudway and Grant Gallicho, "An Interview with Cardinal Walter Kasper," *Commonweal*, May 7, 2014.

back to the convent with an expression of profound peace. For her, even a seemingly perfect marriage is not a recipe for true happiness. The secular filmmaker conveys, in an extraordinarily beautiful and powerful way, the sense of hollowness and weariness that a human spousal relationship evokes in a heart designated to be Christ's alone.

Celibacy and Marriage Are Mutually Supportive, Not Competitive

> It is not a matter of diminishing the value of matrimony in favor of continence.... There is no basis for playing one off against the other.[44]

> Just as virginity receives from physical motherhood the insight that there is no Christian vocation except in the concrete gift of oneself to the other, so physical motherhood receives from virginity an insight into its fundamentally spiritual dimension: it is in not being content only to give physical life that the other truly comes into existence. This means that motherhood can find forms of full realization also where there is no physical procreation.[45]

Just as the sustenance of our planet depends on marriage and parenthood, celibates and married couples also are existentially dependent upon one another. Celibates and married couples both operate from a place of self-giving, the fruit of which is parenthood, either physical or spiritual.

[44] John Paul II, General Audience, April 14, 1982.

[45] Joseph Cardinal Ratzinger, "Letter to the Bishops of the Catholic Church on the Collaboration of Men and Women in the Church and in the World," May 31, 2004.

The daily struggles inherent in marriage and family provide fertile ground for charity. Through acts of charity big and small, married persons constantly give something of themselves. Celibacy, too, helps us understand charity. Celibates must hold a high view of married life in order to make their sacrifice to God important and spiritually fruitful.

Preacher of the papal household Fr. Raniero Cantalamessa, O.F.M. Cap., suggests that the witness of celibacy serves marriage by liberating it from the

> unbearable weight of having to be "everything" for the other, of taking the place of God. The eschatological reservations that virginity [and celibacy] places upon marriage do not lessen its joy; rather, they save it from despair, because they open up for marriage a horizon stretching even beyond death.[46]

For some, marriage and family have become idols, the absolute measure of success. But marriage cannot easily support such high expectations. Nothing human, even something as good as marriage and family, can fully satisfy the human heart.

The real antagonist to holy marriage is not celibacy but, rather, sex that excludes procreation; it creates egoism. And the real antagonist to holy celibacy is forgoing a human spouse and family simply as a means to flee self-sacrifice; it also creates egoism.

On a more speculative note, might celibacy for the Kingdom, in all its rich variations, serve as a defensive shield against the diabolical attacks on marriage and the family that Satan is fiercely waging today? According to Sr. Lucia, one of the divine messages from Our Lady of Fatima was about the last battle on earth before

[46] Raniero Cantalamessa, O.F.M. Cap., *Virginity: A Positive Approach to Celibacy for the Sake of the Kingdom of Heaven* (Staten Island: Society of St. Paul, 1995), 8–9.

Christ's final coming. This battle would be waged against the family. What could be better than an army of celibate souls, espoused to Christ, to defend temporal marriage through accompaniment, prayer, fasting, charitable outreach, and political action?

Celibacy Makes One Free for an Undivided Love of God and for Apostolic Work

> An unmarried woman or a virgin is anxious about the things of the Lord, so that she may be holy in both body and spirit. A married woman, on the other hand, is anxious about the things of the world, how she may please her husband. (1 Cor. 7:34)

> Those who are celibate are de facto freer of ties of affection and have greater freedom of movement to dedicate themselves permanently to conducting and supporting apostolic undertakings. This is also true in the lay apostolate."[47]

The obvious, if not superficial, view of lay celibacy is that it is a vocation that frees one to do more apostolic work, to be more active for others and for the Church. This way of thinking finds a particularly comfortable home among can-do Americans. Indeed, the broad array of charitable organizations in America speaks to the extraordinary fruits of active apostolic work performed by priests, religious, and laypeople since the country's founding.

Just as religious sisters courageously and fearlessly built up much of the Church's educational and health infrastructure, so, too, did single, secular women have a dramatic impact on America.

[47] "Women and Social Life in the Church," no. 92, in *Conversations with Monsignor Escrivá de Balaguer*, http://www.escrivaworks.org/book/conversations-point-92.htm.

Marriage rates for middle-class women on the East Coast plunged in the later part of the nineteenth century, owing to the casualties of the Civil War and the lure of the American West for able-bodied men. Many of these educated single women threw themselves into community service and political reform movements such as abolition and suffrage. Susan B. Anthony, Sarah Moore Grimké, Jane Addams, Alice Paul, Catharine Beecher, and Elizabeth Blackwell, to name just a few, were all single.

Not to diminish the temporal achievements of secular singles past or present, but the important thing is not the mere time made available by not marrying, but a heart fully available for Christ. It is this that makes a person more fruitful in the spiritual realm than in even an admirable social service. Moreover, the potential downside to a singular focus on greater availability for active apostolate is pride. As Pope Benedict XVI warns:

> The solely pragmatic reasons [for celibacy], the reference to greater availability, is not enough: such a greater availability of time could easily become also a form of egoism that saves a person from the sacrifices and efforts demanded by the reciprocal acceptance and forbearance in matrimony; thus, it could lead to a spiritual impoverishment or to hardening of the heart.[48]

Celibacy Is Fruitful

> This perfect continence, out of desire for the kingdom of heaven, has always been held in particular honor in the Church. The reason for this was and is that perfect continence

[48] Address of His Holiness Benedict XVI to the members of the Roman Curia at the traditional exchange of Christmas greetings, December 22, 2006.

> for the love of God is an incentive to charity, and is certainly a particular source of spiritual fecundity in the world.[49]

> Virginity is really the whole offering of soul and body to be consumed in the fire of love and changed into the flame of its glory.[50]

Celibacy, or perfect chastity, can be profoundly powerful and yield great fruits because it is based on great love. God's love for us is infinite, but we are capable of loving only in a finite way. The greatest expression of finite human love is to give one's life for another. This is why martyrs deserve our deepest veneration and why the Church canonizes martyrs so readily. Martyrdom is a radical expression of love for God that may be thrust upon us, as we do not actively seek it. In contrast, celibacy is a radical expression of our love for God, over which we have more control. We are called to perfect chastity, but we also choose it. Celibacy pushes against the outer limits of our capacity to love God.

For priests, celibacy is "a way of ensuring a deeper configuration with Christ."[51] And while "the quality of the priest's identification with Christ does not have an impact on the validity of the celebrated sacraments . . . it does have an impact on their fecundity."[52] The more we love and sacrifice out of love, the greater the spiritual fruits. The extraordinary fruitfulness of celibacy finds its highest expression in the Virgin Mary. She is the Mother of God because

[49] Second Vatican Council, Constitution on the Church *Lumen Gentium* (November 21, 1964), no. 42.

[50] Caryll Houselander, *The Reed of God* (Notre Dame, IN: Ave Maria Press, 2006), 17.

[51] Wojciech Giertych, O.P., "Prayer and Celibacy: The Apostolic Origin of Priestly Celibacy," *The Priest*, September 2011, 87.

[52] Ibid.

she gave the total gift of herself, body and soul, to God. Celibates for the Kingdom, who similarly give the gift of their bodies and souls to God, express a spiritual maternity or paternity that can generate as many descendants as the stars in the sky.

Being continent either by default or for natural reasons is a good thing, just as sorrow for one's sins out of fear of Hell is a good thing. But how much more pleasing to God is sorrow for one's sins out of love for Him, out of a deep regret for hurting one's beloved. In a similar way, responding to the call of celibacy as a means to draw closer to God is a different, much better thing altogether.

Many of us have been taught correctly that love is an act of the will, not an emotion. The risk of this formulation is that it may feed into the mistaken notion that loving others is primarily about doing good works (very American), acting in a virtuous way, or sacrificing for others. Acts of kindness and sacrifice, however, are not the foundation of charity. At its root, charity is friendship with God and embracing others in light of that friendship with God, made possible by Christ — wanting first and foremost for others to become saints, because that is what God wants. Those who develop a deeper fellowship with God, which often is expressed through the voluntary gift of celibacy, may love in a supernaturally more fruitful way than others. This is why Catholics see cloistered nuns as potentially wielding more power than the richest of secular NGOs working to alleviate poverty in the world.

Lay celibacy is potentially an extraordinarily fruitful vocation, but it is also one that is rejected, scorned, or underappreciated; this is sad, because God specially calls certain souls exclusively to Himself. If the life of perfect chastity is not fruitful, then it is not being properly lived. Instead, it can be barren and off-putting. There is the danger of celibacy leading to a negative quality, an impotence that is both physical and spiritual:

Unfortunately, there are not only wise virgins in this world but unwise ones, foolish virgins; and the foolish virgins make more noise in the world than the wise, giving a false impression of virginity by their loveless and joyless attitude to life.... These foolish virgins, like their prototypes, have no oil in their lamps. And no one can give them this oil, for it is the potency of life, the will and capacity to love.[53]

Celibacy, a Foreshadowing of Heaven

Those who are deemed worthy to attain to the coming age and to the resurrection of the dead neither marry nor are given in marriage.... They are like angels; and they are the children of God because they are the ones who will rise. (Luke 20:35–36)

Whatever the bridegroom gives to his friends—trust, confidence, responsibilities—it is to his wife that he gives his name, so that she may be what he is, may do what he does, and so that he may transmit his own life through her.... To be bride is to go constantly from the night of the theological mystery of Love out to the world."[54]

We become what we love and who we love shapes what we become. If we love things, we become a thing. If we love nothing, we become nothing. Imitation is not a literal mimicking of Christ; rather it means becoming the image of the beloved, an image disclosed through transformation. This means we are to become vessels of God's compassionate love for others."[55]

[53] Houselander, *The Reed of God*, 16.

[54] Venerable Madeleine Delbrêl.

[55] St. Clare of Assisi.

Those in heaven enjoy all-encompassing union with God. Celibacy for the express purpose of directing one's entire heart and body to God while here on earth provides a jump-start to heavenly union. Through baptism, we are each called to love God with all our heart, soul, mind, and strength. Celibacy shines a light on the radical meaning of this, our baptismal vocation. Celibacy highlights in a concrete and practical way the truth that only God can fulfill us.

Marriage is the joining of two into one. It is the most intense human union possible. So rich in meaning is the spousal union that God's relationship with His chosen people, the Israelites, and Christ's relationship with His Church are described in spousal terms. Holy Scripture—perhaps nowhere better exemplified than in the Song of Songs—is filled with beautiful spousal language describing the intensity and all-consuming nature of God's relationship with His creation.

Each of us, as baptized Christians, has a spousal relationship with Christ, most intensely and physically realized when we receive Jesus Christ in the Holy Eucharist. We literally become one with Christ at that moment. How important, then, that we unite ourselves to Jesus in the Eucharist fully prepared, "wearing" our finest wedding garment, a pure heart. We do not want to be thrown out of the wedding feast by the angry King (see Matt. 22:12–13)!

A close, holy friend of mine recently made a permanent, private vow to give herself fully to Christ. Her spiritual journey has been a great inspiration to me, especially the way in which she has embraced her spousal relationship with the Lord. She glows and thrives as a bride of Christ. This friend views her relationship with Christ as a sort of engagement before her actual wedding:

> I believe that my wedding day will actually be when I depart from this life and when He comes to take me to Himself, as

> promised.... So you see, I am preparing for that wedding day, by asking and seeking and learning from Our Blessed Mother and the saints how to be most pleasing to God! How to make my Divine Spouse most happy and pleased when He sees me! Perhaps we can make Our Lord cry for joy when He sees us on our wedding day!![56]

Human marriages end at death. Spiritual betrothals to Christ on earth come to their full fruition in heaven. My friend looks toward her death as the moment when she will get to see her spouse face-to-face. This is when the real fun of her marriage begins.

Celibates as Today's Feminists

"Virginity refutes any attempt to enclose women in mere biological destiny."[57] A woman's biological destiny is to bear children. God created women to be maternal whether it be manifested in physical or spiritual maternity. Historically women "broke free" of *physical* childbearing, their biological destiny, through virginity or celibacy, generally as members of a religious order. Lived well, celibacy for Christ bears spiritual offspring.

Today, there is no shortage of artificial and violent means available for women to "escape" their biological destiny. But these means to control fertility have harmed women, emotionally and physically, no less than they have wounded men. Artificial birth control is an ersatz escape and abortion a deadly one. Virginity and celibacy, on the other hand, represent a powerful, spiritual antidote to this Gnostic attempt to "break free" of one's biology.

The feminist movement achieved important gains for women in the late nineteenth and early twentieth centuries, such as voting,

[56] Susan Conroy, private e-mail.

[57] Ratzinger, "Letter on the Collaboration."

property, and contract rights. Over the past half century, women continued to push for, and largely achieved, equality of opportunity in the educational, political, cultural, and economic realms. These welcome and laudable achievements have helped women to develop their talents and to flourish, and today women can enter spheres they never could before. Some of these spheres require many years of study, highly focused work, and extensive travel, which do not easily lend themselves to the raising of a family, as hard as this is for many to accept. It is fitting and potentially spiritually fruitful for dedicated singles to make present the gospel values in these spheres in a particularly feminine way.

Unfortunately, the organized feminist movement, which has been co-opted by the sexual revolution over the past half century, has disempowered women in two ways. First, it has enabled, if not encouraged, men to treat women as objects in service of their own sexual gratification without obligation or commitment. Birth control is ubiquitous, yet more than 40 percent of children in the United States are born to single mothers. Some one million abortions are performed in the United States yearly, and nearly 20 percent of pregnancies end in abortion. Record numbers of women (and men) are medicated. How do these alarming statistics reflect empowered women?

Second, modern feminism has (perhaps) unwittingly endorsed economic norms that generally do not support a woman's flourishing. Some jobs do not lend themselves to a work-life balance supportive of family life. Many work environments, however, are unnecessarily designed in a way that forces women to choose either work or children and a healthy family life. Instead of pushing back, many well-meaning women have fed anti-family structures through the artificial escape route. Some instructive quotes from Sheryl Sandberg's best-selling book, *Lean In*, speak to this desire to force an escape from biological destiny:

> Even if mothers are more naturally inclined toward nurturing, fathers can match that skill with knowledge and effort. As Gloria Steinem once observed, "It's not about biology, but about consciousness." ... So even if "mother knows best" is rooted in biology, it need not be written in stone.... Study after study suggests that the pressure society places on women to stay home and do "what's right for the child" is based on emotion, not evidence.[58]

A word of caution: freely choosing to eschew marriage and motherhood for a life of unencumbered "freedom from biological destiny" to pursue a career is not a recipe for happiness. In the early 1930s, Edith Stein warned, "The lot of more and more women today is to lead a solitary life in the world. Whether they pursue a profession only to earn a living or to lose themselves in work ... it is in the long run a grueling, exhausting struggle."[59]

A women's emotional destiny is to accompany others. Women were created for companionship.[60] So while virginity or celibacy

[58] Sheryl Sandberg, *Lean In: Women, Work, and the Will to Lead* (New York: Alfred A. Knopf, 2013), 108, 135.

[59] Edith Stein, *Essays on Woman* (Washington, D.C.: ICS Publications, 1996), 267.

[60] Nicole Echivard, *Femme, Qui Es-Tu?* (Paris: Criterion, 1985). This is a profound book that delves into the respective natures of man and women based on the Creation narrative. Echivard writes, "Ce que est premier dans l'ordre d'intention est dernier dans l'ordre d'execution," or "The first in the order of intention is the last in the order of creation," suggesting that God had planned to create Eve even before Adam. Indeed, take a look at Michelangelo's Sistine Chapel ceiling fresco of the creation of man. Eve is tucked under God's left arm as He extends the spark of life to Adam. According to Echivard, Eve was created to overcome the solitude of Adam. In a talk titled "The Human Vocation: Being Icons of The Icon," Fr. Wojciech Giertych, O.P.,

frees a woman from biological destiny, it is imperative that she who is made for union give herself away. It is hard to imagine a more powerful sign of the exalted value of a woman than a religious or lay celibate chosen by Christ to love and accompany Him. This is feminism at its best.

---

suggests that this mission to accompany man takes precedence *even over the women's procreative role*.

Chapter 5

Single by Default

Lord, I asked you that I might encounter a great love so as to give meaning to my life. You gave me the grace of being able to believe in the goodness of the human heart and the desire to share that faith with all the badly loved persons whom you made me meet.[61]

Singles suffer the most; they suffer loneliness and judgement, social martyrdom.[62]

Loneliness is the fundamental force that urges mystics to a deeper union with God. For such people, loneliness has become intolerable. But, instead of slipping into apathy or anger, they use the energy of loneliness to seek God. . . . Loneliness, then, can be a force for good.[63]

What about those who are single by default—those who, due to external circumstances and no fault of their own, are prevented from marrying or joining a religious order? Or those who, due to personal circumstances, are unable to do so? What about those who feel called to marriage but do not find a suitable spouse? What

[61] Based on a prayer composed by a Confederate soldier during the Civil War.

[62] Fr. Jacques Philippe in a private conversation to a few single friends.

[63] Jean Vanier, *Becoming Human* (New York, Paulist Press, 1998), 8.

about those with same-sex attraction or the divorced or widowed? And, increasingly common today, what about those who just can't seem to discern God's will for them? Are these souls doomed to lead vocationally bereft lives?

There are a number of reasons why people today do not commit as readily to a state of life or a stable vocation as people did in the past. Younger people today generally are less equipped to discern the quiet promptings of the Holy Spirit and to respond decisively and definitively to those promptings. Society has become fluid, offering a paralyzing plethora of choices; children are coddled, with parents making even the smallest decisions for them; social media and frenetic activity have replaced precious silence and solitude, the necessary air for discernment. The diminished ability to discern and make decisions, combined with the socioeconomic forces at play, help one to understand why there are so many "default" singles in our society today.

With clarity, depth, and pastoral sensitivity, Fr. Wojciech Giertych described the status of today's singles this way:

> There are those who are single, not because they have made some profession, but only because "a good man is hard to come by." They would marry, had somebody proposed.... They live as single laypeople, living out the graces of baptism and the common priesthood of the faithful. And they can have some apostolate according to their own choice and generosity. Their specific way of life is not necessarily intended to be permanent, even though it sometimes turns out to be permanent. They can also be *saints*. [64]

A yearning, unsettled heart is the tasteless, if not bitter, fruit of living out one's entire life in a perpetual default state. An extremely

[64] Wojciech Giertych, O.P., private e-mail, emphasis in original.

bright, thoughtful single friend with a deep faith, who serves the Church beautifully, wrote these insightful words after a discussion we had about being single Catholics:

> Most of the single women I know are single by default. Most of them have not made any kind of permanent vows or commitment, but continue to live out their single life faithfully, as it was given, and as best they can. They aspire to be saints. But I think something important to highlight here is the sense in which there is an absence—at least for most of us, and that is true for me.[65]

Where is God in all of this? I quote at length here a heart-wrenching comment posted online by a woman in response to an article about whether there is a legitimate vocation to the single life:

> What is God's plan and purpose in placing this longing [for marriage] so deeply and fully in my heart—and then, as far as I can see, standing silent during years of tearful prayers begging for that longing to be fulfilled? What might His purpose be in that? What is the purpose in giving me both the faith that leads me to see marriage as the Church understands it, as something beautiful, and also the faith that, over and over, leads to painful rejection in a world that sees relationships very differently? I just don't understand.
>
> Wonderful Catholic friends who I know care about me have suggested that maybe I am called by God to the single life. I like your notion that there is no such calling, because that prospect terrifies me. I don't want to be called to a single life as such, because I have experienced that life only

[65] E-mail from a friend.

> as misery. So I have tried, also over these years, asking God: "Okay, maybe you don't intend a husband for me. What do you want instead? What is this other vocation you have in mind for me?"[66]

Does God call someone to marriage and then leave that person high and dry without a spouse, despite the person's best efforts to find a spouse? Does God "make" someone attracted to the same sex and then say, "Sorry, you have no vocation?" God orders all things "mightily and sweetly" (see Wisd. 8:1), and as Jesus assures us, "Nothing in your life is foreign to My plan for you: everything you have done, every place you have ever been, every person with whom you have been or are connected, is part of My design for your life."[67] Good and admirable desires of the heart, such as marriage or a religious vocation, that are not realized have a purpose in God's guiding of a soul. Might this disappointment serve as a painful sacrifice, a means to increase merits for eternity? Might it be the means God has chosen for such a person to be a great saint in the world? Or might the good and admirable desire of marriage or religious life not be *God's* desire?

In a locution to a Benedictine Monk, Jesus tells us:

> A troubled heart is always an indication of one's lack of trust in Me. Trouble, interior disquiet, comes from wanting to control and manage the things that are better left to My Father's providence.... Let go of the things that you cling to most tightly. Come to Me with empty hands. Hold on to nothing, not even to your own plans and desires for good

[66] Anonymous online comment in response to Mgsr. Charles Pope's article "Is There a Vocation to Single Life? I Think Not and Here's Why,"*Community in Mission*, May 26, 2015.

[67] A Benedictine Monk, *In Sinu Jesu: When Heart Speaks to Heart* (Kettering, OH: Angelico Press, 2016), 257.

> things. If the things that you want for yourself are good, know, beyond any doubt, that the things I want for you are infinitely better.[68]

It's through our faults and less-than-ideal circumstances that God shows His mercy. We should not be idealistic with ourselves. God operates in the world through our humble cooperation, despite our weaknesses.

Humans have a deep hunger to be acknowledged by someone else. Fr. Jacques Philippe writes poignantly about identity and the search for social recognition: "And so we face this paradox: a cruel hunger for recognition and esteem at a time when there is no one in the position to confer them."[69] Our need for recognition today often expresses itself through an extreme, soul-killing obsession with romantic love or sex. But even the ideal of romantic love and marriage, à la Jane Austin's Darcy and Elizabeth, cannot satisfy the recognition we crave. Only God can. No one, no matter how "perfect," can fully satisfy the human heart, which has an insatiable, though not always understood, desire for God. And accessing one's true identity from which this longing for God springs is not easy. Peeling away the superficial and deformed layers to get to the holy core of our personality, where God's love for us burns, is a painful process that requires humility and receptivity to grace.

Reading about the blights that befall Job makes us cringe. At first blush, God comes off as cruel by letting Satan wreak havoc on "blameless and upright" Job. God permits bad things to happen to Job to prove to Satan that Job's devotion is not superficial. God knows the depths of Job's faith, and, indeed, Job passes the test with flying colors. To love God wholeheartedly, like Job, when

[68] Ibid., 260.

[69] Jacques Philippe, *Fire & Light: Learning to Receive the Gift of God*, (New York: Scepter Publishers, 2016), 86.

life doesn't unfold in a desired way is heroic. To embrace God's will in all circumstances requires great faith, the faith of Job. But only by accepting all that life hands us will we truly be at peace. In the end, Job gains an understanding of why he went through great trials. We ourselves might not gain such an understanding while on earth. But very often we come to understand the divine wisdom behind our trials, eventually coming to appreciate how our greatest disappointments are often our greatest blessings. Job's friends mocked and scorned him for his misfortune. But in the end, it was Job's friends whom God chastised, and it was Job who served as an intercessor for those friends.

Sins and imperfections hurt us and show our disrespect for God. But because God gave us free will, He permits sins and imperfections, even though He wills only the good. He permits suffering to occur, knowing that good can come of it. God wills that we be holy, that we open ourselves up to His grace in order to bring us into union with Him, ultimately in heaven, but also here on earth. For some of us, good health may lead to sin and the loss of sanctifying grace. In such a case, God may mercifully permit or even ordain that our health fail in order to save our souls.

Could it be that for certain souls, both marriage and religious life would lead to sin or, at minimum, not be the best means for their sanctification? Many religious orders have shed their habits, their community prayer lives, their identities, and their obedience to Church teachings. Might God be calling fewer women to traditional religious life today than in eras past? Well over 65 percent of men, including Christian men, regularly watch pornography. Sexual aggression is rampant, and fewer men and women are fit to enter sacramental marriages today. Might God be calling fewer people to marriage? Or has the moral landscape rendered many people unable to hear God's call or caused them to reject the vocations to which God is calling them?

Alternatively, might God be calling more men and women out of today's cultural morass to lives permanently dedicated to Him as dedicated singles to leaven today's world from within, similar to the role that members of secular institutes play? If more were aware of this potential path to holiness, might more listen and heed this call? I think that what Pope John Paul II said of secular institutes applies also to dedicated singles:

> This vocation, so timely and I would say so urgent, has to be known and made known.... It is a demanding vocation, because it means bringing the commitments implicit in baptism to their most complete fulfillment in evangelical radicalism, and also because this evangelical life must be incarnated in a wide variety of situations.[70]

We are hardwired to give ourselves away. God made us for union: "It is not good for the man to be alone" (Gen. 2:18). Keeping one's heart for oneself results in unsettledness, perpetual searching, a lack of peace. Profound peace and joy are the sweet fruits of uniting oneself to another, whether the other be a virtuous spouse in a sacramental marriage or God Himself. Pope Benedict proclaimed these encouraging words about firmly committing oneself to another: "Can man bind himself forever? Can he say a 'yes' for his whole life? Yes, he can. He was created for this."[71]

Church history is replete with examples of holy single souls wholeheartedly dedicated to Christ while living in the world—Catherine of Siena, Rose of Lima, Margaret of Castello, Guiseppe Moscati, Madeleine Delbrêl, Caryll Houselander, Pauline-Marie

[70] *Words of Inspiration: The Private Prayers of Pope John Paul II* (New York: Simon and Schuster, 2001), 13.

[71] Benedict XVI, the traditional exchange of Christmas greetings, December 22, 2006.

Jaricot, Gemma Galgani, Joan d'Arc, Pierre Toussaint, Germaine Cousin, Benedict Joseph Labre — not to mention the many virgins who forsook marriage in the early Church. These saints and venerables bucked the norms of their more rigidly structured social milieus. Although certain elements of modern culture have made vocational decision-making more difficult, today's fluid society may be just the sort of environment that more naturally allows, if not calls for, more dedicated single vocations.

We know that "all things work for good for those who love God" (Rom. 8:28). Who is to say that "all things" are just pleasant things? "All things" may be a rejected call to the religious state, not finding an appropriate spouse, or some other condition that prevents entrance to the religious or married states. But such circumstances may ultimately lead one to a life of sanctity in the lay state as a dedicated single, singularly focused on Christ. Perhaps, for these beloved souls, God makes something inherently bad into something good. God never sends us crosses we cannot handle. I think God sends more consolations to those who accept or, better yet, embrace their crosses. The bigger our crosses, the closer Jesus is to us, ready to share our burdens, if we only let Him. There is much pain and suffering in the world today. Jesus wants to share, alleviate, and sanctify this suffering, but He needs receptive hearts to do His work. Souls who suffer the most are closest to His precious heart. And souls who shut Him out make Him suffer dearly.

Rather than focusing on what we do not have, a human spouse or a religious vocation, we would be better served to focus on the extraordinary opportunity we've been given: time and an unencumbered heart to think about and converse with Jesus frequently. It is time spent in prayer or making acts of faith that help us exercise the virtues, especially patience and humility. Sanctity consists in the meeting of human frailty with the power of God. Easier written than done, but if we confidently ask Jesus to shift our thinking by first asking Him to embrace our cross for us until we are able to embrace it willingly, then it does become easy. It truly becomes a cause for rejoicing.

Chapter 6

Single for a Greater Purpose

In Him we were also chosen, destined in accord with the purpose of the One who accomplishes all things according to the intention of His will, so that we might exist for the praise of His glory, we who first hoped in Christ.

—Ephesians 1:11–12

Find your delight in the Lord who will give you your heart's desire.

—Psalm 37:4

Oh, let us love our vocation and strive to persevere in it! Then everything will be all right with us.

—Blessed Francis Xavier Seelos

If we discern that God is calling us exclusively to Himself in the world and we respond with a decisive, permanent commitment to embrace Christ in return, then this is a true and admirable vocation. The foundation of a godly vocation is the gift of self, a dying to self that bears spiritual fruits.

I think that many today are responding to a call to dedicate themselves wholeheartedly to Christ and to spread His truth in the increasingly complex world of politics, business, culture, science, mass media, and education. Our temporal skills and undivided focus play a role in this evangelization, but only a minor one. The major role is played by Christ. If we allow it, we serve as the conduits making Jesus visible to others. Jesus speaks, comforts, heals, and draws others to the Father in the Holy Spirit through us.

Many whom God may be calling to dedicate themselves exclusively to Him in the world, however, are not responding. Perhaps this is because few realize that this is an option, or, perhaps, some are holding back, continuing to seek human spouses even though this may not be God's will.

I think God may be calling more of us to serve Him as dedicated singles precisely because it flies in the face of an increasingly licentious and hyperactive culture. Joyful lay celibates witness to the underappreciated virtue of purity.

Might dedicated singles serve as antidotes to frenetic activity? Fr. Donald Haggerty provocatively suggests that it is the tepidity of priests and religious—by living distracted lives and treating prayer as an obligation—that fails to attract more souls to Christ.[72] This warning against distracted, tepid lives applies equally to the laity, not just to those who attend Mass only on Christmas and Easter but also to the stalwart, daily communicants and to those who are great apostolic organizers. Are they effective evangelizers? "So much done visibly in the Church is futile in the supernatural realm because no serious prayer lies behind it," writes Fr. Haggerty.[73] Pulling no punches, he goes on, "It is easy to seek one's own glory, and religion has always provided fine opportunities.... Often enough in the Church there are appealing projects that disguise spiritual emptiness behind gloss and a glittering façade, but only temporarily."[74]

[72] Donald Haggerty, *Conversion: Spiritual Insights into an Essential Encounter with God*, (San Francisco, Ignatius Press, 2017), 174.

[73] Ibid., 176.

[74] Ibid., 178.

"Gloss and a glittering façade" is not the description that comes to mind as it relates to the dedicated-single vocation. It is a hidden, humble, misunderstood, underappreciated vocation. It is a vocation that best corresponds to those thirty hidden years of Jesus before the three years of His public ministry. It is a vocation that allows one to spend countless hours alone with Jesus in front of the tabernacle or behind closed doors. It also allows for countless hours in external apostolic activity, works of mercy, or advancement in an edifying career. But it is the extended periods of prayer and the depth of the personal relationship with Jesus that make a well-lived dedicated-single vocation so potentially fruitful.

Might God be calling more to live solitary lives in the proverbial desert? John the Baptist's mother and father each descended from high-priestly stock; his father was an esteemed Temple priest. So Bishop Barron asks, "Why is this son of a priest not working in the Temple?" And, "Why are the people going out from Jerusalem to commune with him?" In another provocative comment about institutional religious life, Bishop Barron says:

> The answer to the first is that he is engaging in a prophetic critique of a Temple that has gone bad. And the answer to the second is that he is performing the acts of a purified Temple priest out in the desert. His baptism was a ritual cleansing and a spur to repent, precisely what a pious Jew would have sought in the Temple.[75]

First and foremost, someone called to a dedicated-single vocation is called to the lay state. And the laity are called to work *in* the world, as compared with the clergy or traditional religious orders, who are called to bring Christ to the world from *outside* the world.

[75] Advent Gospel Reflections, December 19, 2018, https://adventreflections.com/advent-day-18/.

The vows made by religious and clergy necessarily uproot them from secular structures; at least they *should*. In contrast, laypersons are necessarily rooted in secular relationships and structures; they live out intimate daily contact with others in their families, social circles, and professional milieus:

> But the laity, by their very vocation, seek the kingdom of God by engaging in temporal affairs and by ordering them according to the plan of God. They live in the world, that is, in each and in all of the secular professions and occupations. They live in the ordinary circumstances of family and social life, from which the very web of their existence is woven.[76]

Laypeople wield the power of Christ primarily through silent faith and charity rather than through the proclamation of doctrine. They sanctify the world through authentic, grace-filled lives in concrete, everyday circumstances. The *invisible* yeast of the gospel touches the world in devout laypeople, not in *visible* ecclesial positions or institutes.

The glory of God and the salvation of one's soul are the only safe criteria for discerning and responding to this dedicated-single vocation of "holy liberty." Understanding underlying motives is critical to the discernment of any vocation but especially so for the dedicated-single vocation, which can easily be embraced for the wrong reasons. If the single life is chosen primarily for freedom or pleasure, sanctification is much harder, if not impossible, to achieve.

Good motives for embracing the dedicated-single vocation include plenty of quiet time for prayer to deepen one's relationship with God, even for those dedicated to active apostolate, helping

[76] *Lumen Gentium*, 31.

family and friends, or the pursuit of an academic or professional career:

> Many people who are unmarried are not only devoted to their own family but often render great service in their group of friends, in the Church community, and in their professional lives. Sometimes their presence and contributions are overlooked, causing in them a sense of isolation. Many put their talents at the service of the Christian community through charity and volunteer work. Others remain unmarried because they consecrate their lives to the love of Christ and neighbor. Their dedication greatly enriches the family, the Church, and society.[77]

It may be that the single life is simply the best way to achieve sanctity for a particular personality type or constitution. No one knows us better than God does. He knows our strengths and weaknesses, our deep desires and how they may best be fulfilled.

From all eternity, God has had a particular plan for each of His children based on the gifts and circumstances that He has provided. Creation is rich in diversity, as is the Church: "As a body is one though it has many parts, and all the parts of the body, though many, are one body, so also Christ" (1 Cor. 12:12). We all have the same origin and the same destiny, but we each have a unique role to play here on earth.

Hans Urs von Balthasar has little positive to say about single laity in his opus *The Christian State of Life*, but he does make an exception for those to whom God has bestowed certain natural gifts to be deployed in service to the Kingdom. Balthasar cites the Old Testament example of Bezalel. God tells Moses:

[77] Pope Francis, *Amoris Laetitia*, no. 158.

> See, I have chosen Bezalel … and I have filled him with a divine spirit of skill and understanding and knowledge in every craft: in the production of embroidery, in making things of gold, silver, or bronze, in cutting and mounting precious stones. (Exod. 31:2–5)

Stewarding his special gifts, according to Balthasar, demands that Bezalel be single "in a kind of holy madness, which consumes his whole life and all his senses in the service of an art that is itself a service of God—so that the individual may remain unmarried."[78] Might dedicated singles leading apostolates, writing, producing art, teaching, or influencing public policy be today's Bezalels?[79]

[78] Balthasar, *The Christian State of Life*, 424.

[79] In an exceedingly helpful analysis of the relevance of Balthasar's comments about Bezalel to dedicated singles, Patricia Sullivan writes, "While respecting his insistence that Bezalel does not provide a model for the foundation of a state of Christian life, Balthasar's theology of Bezalel implicitly suggests that the basic Christian principle of stewardship is a guide for the process of discernment about how one should live the Christian vocation in one's particular, personal way. Therefore, Balthasar's theology offers a vocational guide that can be especially valuable for laypersons who believe that they may be suited to nonvowed single Christian life. Lacking the 'differentiated call' to religious life, and without clear providential direction toward any other particular state or form of life, the story of Bezalel challenges those contemplating life as laypersons to consider which form of the lay state will allow them best to put their gifts to use for the service or God, Church, and world." "The Nonvowed Form of the Lay State," 335. Earlier, Sullivan suggests, "The single nonvowed Catholic who did not deliberately renounce marriage might examine whether or not divine providence placed him or her in the secular single life because his or her gifts could be employed in God's service more completely there than elsewhere." Ibid., 333.

For a special mission or apostolate to generate supernatural fruits, time for stillness to listen to God is a necessary precondition. To pave the way for Christ, John the Baptist spent his adult life in the desert. Christ spent thirty years in obscurity and forty days in the desert before His three years of public ministry. St. Paul spent three years in quiet study and contemplation in Arabia after his conversion, before his active ministry.

The way I see it, dedicated singles have a greater potential either to become saints or to fall miserably short of what God has created them to be.

Those who discern and embrace God's call to be His alone in world—without a human spouse or the formal structure of religious life—are not necessarily making something inherently bad into something good. Susan Conroy, a dear and holy friend who has taken a private vow of permanent chastity as a means of giving herself more fully to Christ, makes it clear that remaining outwardly single in the world is exactly how God has called her to live:

> We must ardently desire to love and serve God in the way and in the place He wishes! As for me, He sent me back out into the world! While I was literally in the convent doing a "come and see." He essentially made clear to me at the age of 22 that there was some "unfinished work in the world" for me to do; so I left the convent in the South Bronx after my "come and see," and I returned to the world to seek whatever God wished for me to accomplish! And He has kept me out here in the world, on the front lines of the battle, so to speak!

This friend beautifully exemplifies the dedicated-single vocation described by Pope Pius XII:

> [Celibacy] also flourishes among many who are lay people in the full sense: men and women who are not constituted

> in a public state of perfection and yet by private promise or vow completely abstain from marriage and sexual pleasures, in order to serve their neighbor more freely and to be united with God more easily and more closely.[80]

One of the more tempered reactions I received when discussing this book project came from a devout, single Catholic friend over dinner in Rome. He cautioned that a focus on the single lay vocation, not closely tied to an established Church institute or society, could be perceived as a bit Protestant, if not too American. A Catholic view of sanctity places great emphasis on the ecclesial community, relative to the more individualistic approach toward piety inherent in Protestantism. It is not the rare Continental European priest who views American Catholics as swaying a little Protestant.

My friend makes an important cautionary point. A single layperson should proudly exclaim, as did St. Teresa of Avila, "I am a daughter of the Church!" Only in the Catholic Church can we physically receive God in the Eucharist—not a memorial or representation, but the actual Flesh and Blood of God incarnate, Jesus Christ. Only in the Catholic Church can we participate in Christ's redeeming Passion in the Sacrifice of the Mass. Only in the Catholic Church can we participate fully in Christ's Mystical Body on earth. Independence *from* formal structures is not about being freed to do one's "own thing." Rather, it is about being freed for something special, something that God has in mind, requiring availability and flexibility to fulfill within the embrace of the Church.

Catholic mystic, artist, and writer Caryll Houselander was uncomfortable operating within formal ecclesial organizations, which could get "stuck in their own 'charism' and distract [their]

[80] *Sacra Virginitas*, no. 6.

adherents from spontaneously responding to the here and now of daily circumstance."[81] Houselander couldn't be contained within the constraints of organizational boundaries, preferring instead to respond to the promptings of the Holy Spirit in a very personal way.

Three clichés aptly describe those of us called to the dedicated-single vocation. We march to the beat of our own drums. We feel like square pegs who don't quite fit into society's round holes. And we draw outside the lines.

In my early twenties, I worked for a year in Boston. On cold, winter days I would take lunch-break walks, meandering in and out of the atriums of modern, high-rise buildings. On one such day, I came upon a line of people waiting for graphology readings. This unusual event was the brilliantly conceived marketing ploy of a high-end stationary company. Handwriting analysis is more widely embraced in Europe than in the United States, where many consider it a pseudoscience, as ESP is viewed. My curiosity immediately kicked into action, so I queued up. At my turn, I approached the handwriting expert, sat down, and copied a stock phrase on a sheet of fine stationary. My sample evoked quite a reaction from the heretofore bored-looking expert: "You wrote outside the border! Rarely does anyone write outside the border!" Immediately put on the defensive, I stammered something about not being told there was a rule against writing outside the border. I remember none of her comments about my chicken-scratch handwriting, only something about my not being enamored with rules and that I would lead an unusual life.

To the secular world, and even to some religious, living as a dedicated single may seem odd. A Dominican friar said in a homily,

[81] "A Labor of Love: Work and the States of Life," *Humanum: Issues in Family, Culture, and Science* 2 (2017).

"We can become fools for Christ, because He became a fool for us. Like Zacchaeus, Jesus climbed a sycamore tree for us." So much of our faith is seemingly "crazy." Being a dedicated single in order to live more resolutely for this Jesus who climbed a sycamore tree for us seems rather common in comparison.

Few discern a call to lay celibacy when they are young—during high school, college, or early adulthood—when most people discern a call to religious life, the priesthood, or marriage. I think most dedicated singles originally assume that they will get married and then gradually discern that this is not God's call for them. Typically, they sense a strong calling to the lay state, but some come to the dedicated-single vocation after first thinking they have a call to the religious state.

I never felt particularly drawn to religious life; from my earliest memories, I wanted to go forth and conquer the world. I once spent nearly two months living in a community of consecrated women in Mexico, and at that time I was open to entering religious life in a contemplative order, but it just did not feel right for me. When I told this to the superior of one order, she told me that God speaks in whispers (see 1 Kings 19:12). The whispers I heard simply weren't directing me to marriage or to professed religious life.

I had never given a lot of thought to marriage and kids. I do not remember this, but my mother tells me I never played with dolls as a little girl. Animals were my thing. The secular prep school I attended valued academics and self-exploration over dating, and, in college, I was too caught up in my studies and extracurricular activities to date much. I dated quite a few guys after graduate school, but no one with whom I could envision spending my entire life. Frankly, I became bored spending time with a guy after a few months of dating, so I assumed that I had yet to find the "right" one. I also spent nearly a decade working on Wall Street, which kept me busy; I traveled constantly for work and was well paid. But this wasn't the reason I did not get married. I wanted more than what a human man could offer. Relationships left me wistful, with a corner of my heart yearning for something more. Ultimately, I realized that God was not calling me either to marriage or traditional religious life.

Women with intense, "high-flying" careers are often faulted for working so hard that they are not able to meet a potential husband. For me and for many Catholic women I know, this isn't the case. I worked mostly with men, and, in fact, some of the men I dated I met through work. But no one seemed worthy enough to entrust my life to. Another common refrain is that women are too picky or have unrealistic expectations of an ideal spouse. Yes, this is probably the case for some, but it was not my experience or that of many women I know.

I've never focused much on birthdays or on my age; in fact, I often have to think for a moment before recalling my age. Turning forty, however, was hard. It is hard for most unmarried women who want to be married because of the ticking of the biological clock. But it was in my early forties that I began to open up to whatever God had in store for me. Soon after this heartfelt acceptance, it became clear that Jesus was asking, "What about me?" It was an intimidating realization—not the fact that I was not meant to have a human spouse but the idea that Jesus might be calling *me*. I felt a touch of what Our Lady must have felt when the angel Gabriel announced to her that she had been chosen for a special mission. *Me?*

After processing the realization of God's call for me, a profound sense of peace and joy came over me. And even during challenging moments, it has never left me. At the same time, I feel extraordinarily blessed and fortunate to have been chosen by Jesus to be His own, "alone" amid the world, but also infinitely unworthy: "Really, You couldn't have done better, Jesus?"

After I discerned that God was calling me exclusively to Himself, I could understand a bit more how He is a "jealous God" (see Exod. 20:5). I believe that God seeks an especially intimate relationship with many of those whom He calls to be dedicated singles. How did I come to realize this? I suppose it was gradual, until there came a moment when I just knew that God wanted me for Himself and that no man would ever satisfy me. It was not about being too picky. It was about the fact that God is *so* much more than any human, and I so longed for more than what I saw directly before my eyes.

When I contemplated my friend's warning about the single lay vocation potentially leaning too Protestant, I came upon Jean-Baptiste Chautard's powerful book *The Soul of the Apostolate*, a book hailed by popes and saints alike. I think it should be required reading for anyone engaged in apostolic works. Toward the end of the book, Chautard provides a beautiful meditation on the liturgical life. It made me realize that the most important way a Catholic, especially one with a dedicated-single vocation, can truly live as a "daughter of the Church" is to take advantage of the Church's liturgy as a means to come into closer union with God. Chautard defines liturgy as "the public, social, and official worship given by the Church of God."[82] It is how members of the Church express the virtue of religion and, in turn, how she instructs and sanctifies souls.

In a footnote, Chautard quotes the funeral sermon of Maria Theresia of Austria:

> The Church, inspired by God and instructed by the Holy Apostles, has disposed the year in such a way that we may

[82] Jean-Baptiste Chautard, O.C.S.O., *The Soul of the Apostolate* (Charlotte, NC: TAN Books, 2012), 215.

> find in it, together with the life, the mysteries, the preaching and doctrine of Jesus Christ, the true fruit of all these in the admirable virtues of His servants and in the example of His saints, and, finally, a mysterious compendium of the Old and New Testaments and of the whole of Ecclesiastical History.[83]

Praying with others in union with the prayer of the Church brings down special graces, disposes the soul to greater virtue, and makes the heart more pliant to the promptings of the Holy Spirit. It also makes one's prayer more potent, since there are two levels of participation involved in liturgical prayer: the actions of the individual and of the whole body of the Church.

The powerful, timely book *In Sinu Jesu* is a memoir by a Benedictine monk who has received locutions from Jesus Christ and the Blessed Mother. In a locution dated December 3, 2014, Jesus was especially adamant about the importance of praying the Divine Office (Liturgy of the Hours): "Let no one doubt of the singular efficacy of the Divine Office. When the Office ceases in a given place, there the Church has become mute, she has lost her voice; she no longer has the means by which I want her to pour out her heart in My presence."[84]

Why are the psalms, which largely make up the Divine Office, so dear to Jesus? Because, as He expressed to the Benedictine monk, it was through the psalms that "I poured out My own heart to My Father, and in the prayers of David and the holy ones of Israel, My Father heard My voice and inclined to listen to the prayer of My heart."[85]

[83] Ibid., 218–219.

[84] *In Sinu Jesu*, 254.

[85] Ibid., 253.

What a privilege and how powerful for *all* of us, especially for dedicated singles, to recite the divinely inspired prayers of the Church, united to Jesus' own pleading before the Father in Heaven![86]

In another footnote in *The Soul of the Apostolate*, Chautard recounts a powerful tale about St. Ignatius of Loyola:

> Union with somebody else's prayer can lead one to a high degree of prayer! Take the case of the peasant who offered to carry the baggage of St. Ignatius and his companions. When he noticed that, as soon as they arrived at some inn, the Fathers hastened to find some quiet spot and recollect themselves before God, he did as they did, and fell on his knees too. One day they asked him what he did when he thus recollected himself, and he answered: "All I do is say: 'Lord, these men are saints, and I am their packhorse. Whatever they do, I want to be doing too'; and so that is what I offer up to God."

Aren't we all packhorses compared with the angelic words of Sacred Scripture, the Church Fathers, and the saints? Is not "Come to the Table of Plenty" a packhorse compared with "Missa Papae Marcelli"?

[86] Truth be told, I had a hard time figuring out the Divine Office "system," with every feast day dictating some exception. Simple-to-use online resources such as apps and *Magnificat* resolved this difficulty.

Chapter 7

Being Called

Come over to me, all you whose great plans for yourself have failed.
You don't know how lucky you are.
And others too.

— Fr. Thomas Dominic Rover, O.P.

Where does God lead souls that find no secure place in this world but into the desert of the heart? The desert within them is the secret destiny of these souls, not by their own design, but by a divine choice.

—Fr. Donald Haggerty, *Conversion*

Nothing can be more welcome or more readily useful to the Lord for the purposes of His salvific providence than the pure gift of self that renounces every calculation and assessment of its own fruits and looks only to Him, listens to Him, perseveres in availability to Him, and finds satisfaction only in Him.

—Hans Urs von Balthasar, *The Laity and the Life of the Counsels*

I think one of the reasons it took me so long to discern my vocation as a dedicated single was my mistaken belief that, apart from a few "extreme" cases in which God chooses some to be priests or nuns, He treats the rest of us the same—and the default mode of "the same" is marriage.

I think my misperception was spawned by one of the faults of our age—the desire for radical egalitarianism. The ideal of total equality seems admirable in theory. In practice, it causes harm on both the personal and societal levels. Absolute equality goes against God's hierarchical ordering of the universe and against our human nature. It rejects the theological virtue of hope, which has as its object eternal life with God, not perfect equality or justice here on earth. It also leads one to underappreciate the unique love with which God loves each of us and the unique way in which we are each called to conform ourselves to Christ. Politically, egalitarianism run amok led to the past century of terror. Think Russia, Ukraine, China, Cambodia, Venezuela, Cuba, North Korea—and the list goes on.

Conceiving of God in a somewhat abstract, pantheist, Buddhist sort of way also contributed to my initial incredulity at the idea that God might be calling me to Himself. This is another dangerous tendency of our age. From what I see, the idealization of equality and an overly abstract conception of God are errant ways of thinking that have crept into certain corners of the Church.

The truth is that God loves and guides each of us particularly. He does not have some preconceived deterministic plan that we have to fulfill. When we make true choices, God confirms them. We are not all identical flowers planted in a garden. An interesting garden is filled with many types of flowers. Once I grasped this, I was able to embrace the idea that God was calling me to Himself. St. Thérèse of Lisieux compared herself to a pure, white lily that, along with the regal roses, towered over the smaller violets and daisies. The sun shines on *each* and *every* flower, despite its size or shape. Each of us, in our respective spots in the flower garden, basks in the warm glow of God's love.

We do not merit being baptized children of God, our most important vocation, or being members of a priestly race (see 1 Pet.

2:9). Nor do we merit being priests, religious, married persons, or dedicated singles. God chooses. He calls whom He wills.

Of all the people present during Christ's Passion, I relate most to Simon of Cyrene. I was struck by how Mel Gibson portrayed Simon in his film *The Passion of the Christ*. Simon had to be manhandled by the Roman soldiers before he grudgingly agreed to help Jesus carry His Cross. It is an understatement to say that Simon did not initially appreciate the exalted role for which he was specially chosen. And the unruly crowds thronging the road to Calvary were derisive toward Simon throughout the ordeal. Isn't it often like that with us? I cannot count the times I went into a situation kicking and screaming, only to realize later that it was exactly the right thing for me. Our greatest disappointments are often our greatest blessings.

Isn't this how it is for most of us who come to realize that Jesus is calling us for Himself, not in a convent or as part of a religious order but, rather, out in the world without the protection of a like-minded community? Instead, ours is a unique, individualized call, lived out alone, obscurely cleaved to Christ, amid a fantastic array of God's beloved weaklings.

What happened to Simon? Despite his initial resistance, Simon came to know Jesus. Jesus looked into his eyes and filled his heart. Simon was vanquished by a Person and a Love unlike any other. He came to understand and appreciate his vocation as a beloved creature, shoulder to shoulder with his Brother and Redeemer, Jesus Christ. When the unruly crowd mocked Jesus, Simon rose with supernatural courage and defended the Man he had come to love.

One might imagine an elderly Simon reflecting—with great humility, thanksgiving, and amazement—on that extraordinary moment that radically changed his life on earth and for eternity. He was chosen to share in Christ's sufferings in a unique and powerful way. This is how it is for many of us who are called to love and serve Jesus exclusively and as singles. Very few would have chosen to help Jesus carry His Cross solitarily on that hot, dirty road to Calvary. But once fully embraced, this sacrifice has the potential to be extraordinarily fruitful and joy filled. This is why I say that, if it were up to me, Simon of Cyrene would be the patron saint of dedicated singles living in the world.

In contrast, Veronica needed no push to help Jesus endure His agony. She immediately responded to an internal prompting, and good thing she did, as the opportunity to console Jesus was brief. Although many, if not most, dedicated singles take a while to respond to Christ's invitation to be exclusively His, once embraced, our state of life allows us to be more spontaneous, to respond at a moment's notice to the needs of others.

God respects our free choice and waits for us to give ourselves wholly to Him before He gives Himself completely to us. The more completely we give ourselves to God, the more our souls are purified and open to the gifts that God so wants to bestow upon us.

The image that comes to mind is that of a golden key left on the side of a dirt path. Instead of picking up this valuable, though perhaps dusty, key (and perhaps embracing a dedicated single vocation), instead of cherishing it and holding it close to our hearts, we kick it aside. We walk by without appreciating the key's true value. How sad for us, and how sad for the One who placed the key along our path, hoping we would use it to open the door to His Sacred Heart.

Let us *not* be like Hannah, who, though barren, was Elkanah's most beloved spouse. Instead of feeling gratitude and joy for being specially loved by Elkanah, she stewed over what she lacked:

> When the day came for Elkanah to offer sacrifice, he used to give . . . a double portion to Hannah because he loved her, though the Lord had made her barren. . . . Her husband

> Elkanah used to ask her: "Hannah, why do you weep, and why do you refuse to eat? Why do you grieve? Am I not more to you than ten sons?" (1 Sam. 1:4–8)

Learning to Let God Act

"Love does not always heed the desires of those whom it loves," said Augustin Guillerand. We are all called to perfection, but this can be achieved only if we follow the promptings of the Holy Spirit and embrace God's will for us. Conforming our wills to God's will is the key to our sanctification.

I used to think that progress in the moral life required a dramatic struggle between my will and God's will, as if the two wills were on equal footing and were equally free. But they're not equal, and often the human will is not really free, whether we realize it or not. Our wills are truly free and creative only when we choose to act in a good and fitting way. Over time, as we grow in virtue, our choices become united with God's design, often imperceptibly. Our wills then become united with God's will, and this is when we are truly free. God gave us the power to choose so that we could freely choose to love and serve Him.

When we try to impose on God our projects and ideas, we block His will for our lives. These are easy words to write and to grasp intellectually but much harder to live by. I know because I am very strong willed, and it took me years on my knees to understand this truth. It is still a daily struggle but, thanks to God's grace, a slowly diminishing one.

God wants our happiness, as hard as that is, at times, for us to believe. Only by really, fully accepting the unfolding of the circumstances in our lives, under God's loving, watchful direction, will we be happy. Many of us think we have embraced God's will for our lives, but deep down we still cling to our separate plans. A priest once told me that I should be as thankful for something that "goes wrong" as for something that "goes right," since the thing that "goes wrong" could be a part of God's loving plan. "Impossible," was my thinking at the time, but gradually I've started to get the hang of it—except when I'm confronted with heavy traffic, airplane delays, rudeness, incompetence …

Many live in a spiritual holding pattern. They're waiting for something better (perhaps to get married), and this "better" thing is generally what they themselves want. Too often, people take a negative view of their circumstances, when, in fact, those circumstances are God's special pedagogy, directing their way to spiritual growth. By rebelling against the circumstances in which they find themselves, people may be rejecting what God wants for them. This doesn't mean that people should accept or remain in untenable or dangerous situations, of course. God wants only the best for us.

I had always wondered why Jesus waited four days to go to Lazarus after receiving word that his beloved friend was near death (see John 11:1–34). At some point, I realized that Jesus' purposeful delay shows us that He can do so much more with our lives than what we aspire to. "You want a measly healing, Martha? I can raise your brother from death to life!" In a similar way, Jesus calls some to a special lay vocation: "You keep pining for a human spouse? I want you to be *my* beloved spouse on earth."

Fr. Donald Haggerty has another interpretation of the story of Lazarus as it relates to Jesus' tears. Why would Jesus cry at Lazarus' tomb if He knew that He would raise him to life?

> Jesus may have wept from seeing a soul [Mary of Bethany] He especially loved now bent down in tears, refusing to look at Him, cut off and withdrawn, because her request had not been answered to her expectation, even as He intended to fulfill it. Perhaps a flash of divine awareness in Jesus occurred

> at that hour for the many souls in the future who, in loss or tragedy, would indulge similar disappointments toward Him and lose confidence in Him because their expectations would not be answered by God to their liking.[87]

How many souls might Jesus be calling to Himself, to an exclusive relationship with Him, but these souls refuse either because they are not sensitive to His call or because they are too attached to their own plans for themselves? How sad this must make Jesus!

He Leadeth Me, by Fr. Walter Ciszek, S.J., made a big impact on me. It made me appreciate how God tailors His plan for each of us. The culminating, grace-filled moment in Fr. Ciszek's life took place in a Soviet Siberian prison camp, after many years of brutal confinement and long periods of cruel interrogation. Fr. Ciszek became increasingly anxious about his daily interrogation, worried that he would break down and provide incriminating information about his fellow inmates and other priests he knew. One day, he came to his breaking point and cried out to God that he was giving up. He had no more strength to endure the interrogations on his own. It was his white-flag moment. In that moment, great peace came over him. No longer would it be Fr. Ciszek facing the interrogators; it would be Jesus Himself.

Ciszek had always been strong willed and defiant, so much so that his father took the teenage Ciszek to the local police station and begged the officers to arrest his trouble-making son and admit him to reform school to straighten him out. It took twenty years in a Siberian prison camp for Fr. Ciszek to hand over his will to God in a moment that he refers to as his true conversion:

> And the stronger the ingredient of self develops in our lives, the more severe must our humiliations be in order to purify

[87] Haggerty, *Conversion*, 232.

> us.... In that one year of interrogations, these last terrible few hours, the primacy of self that had manifested itself and been reinforcing itself even in methods of prayer and spiritual exercises underwent a purging, through purgatory, that left me cleansed to the bone. It was a pretty hot furnace, to say the least, very nearly as hot as hell itself.[88]

Reading this, I thought, "I want to make this easier. I do not want God to have to permit such pain and strife in order for me to hand over my iron will, so I'd better start praying for the graces to hand it over more easily."

In his wonderful little book *Interior Freedom*, Fr. Jacques Philippe reminds us that the experience of genuine freedom requires acceptance of things we cannot change. He calls it "the paradoxical law of human life," which grows out of the recognition that "one cannot be truly free unless one accepts not always being free."[89] In other words, the times when we cannot control our situations are precisely those moments when we are most likely to mature and become holier.

Control is a big issue, especially for those of us in the developed world. Technological advancements have us believing that we can control practically everything, even the weather. Surrendering to God's will may have been easier before the advent of air conditioning, penicillin, and gender-reassignment surgery.

Fr. Philippe writes that, when faced with circumstances we do not choose, especially when they seem frightening or intrusive, we generally respond in one of three ways. We may rebel, brazenly refusing to heed a summons we did not ask for or are

[88] Walter J. Ciszek, S.J., *He Leadeth Me* (San Francisco: Ignatius Press, 1995), 73–74.

[89] Jacques Philippe, *Interior Freedom* (New York: Scepter Publishers, 2007), 28.

loath to accept. We may resign ourselves, as though powerless, allowing no good fruit to be born. Or, best of all, we may respond with receptivity, leading to real, lasting assent. We can say yes to something that initially seemed negative because we believe that something positive will emerge from it. The virtue of hope exercised in such a receptive gesture — like Joseph's trusting acceptance of the angel's prompting to marry his betrothed, Mary — is what makes the assent so fruitful, so powerful. Fr. Philippe writes, "The great secret of all spiritual fruitfulness and growth is learning to let God act."[90]

Purifying Our Hope

We need to purify our hope in order to grow in God's love and life. Hope is the confident expectation that we will spend eternity with God in inexpressible joy. To hope means to have God as the goal of our lives, rather than anything created, whether it be a job, a spouse, or a relaxing retirement. So much of our spiritual life involves purifying our hope so that it may be entirely oriented toward God. According to St. John of the Cross, purifying our hope also entails purifying our principal emotions — joy, sorrow, and fear.[91] We cannot do this alone; we must ask God for the grace to hope in Him, to fear Him, to find joy in Him, and to be sorrowful over anything that is counter to His plan.

Hope is the most underappreciated theological virtue, I think. It is woefully lacking in today's secular, materialist society. How can an atheist joyfully hope in the idea that, after death, one's body becomes worm food, nothing more? How can one be joyful if hope

[90] Ibid.

[91] St. John of the Cross, *The Ascent of Mount Carmel*, in The Collected Works of St. John of the Cross, trans. Kieran Kavanaugh, O.C.D., and Otilio Rodriguez, O.C.D. (Washington, D.C.: Institute of Carmelite Studies, 1991), 292.

is exclusively wrapped up in meeting a spouse or achieving success at work? Even if these ambitions are achieved, they provide only momentary joy if the primary object of those hopes is not God. Even among many devout Christians, during this unsettled moment in the Church, I see a lack of hope.

If Simon of Cyrene is the patron saint of dedicated singles, then hope is the dedicated single's special theological virtue. I had never given a lot of thought to hope, compared with faith and charity, until I attended Fr. Giertych's course on the theological virtues a few years ago in Rome and listened to him during a retreat in the summer of 2016. He outlined four types of hope.

At its most basic level, hope is a healthy *emotion*. It is the happiness and excitement we feel in thinking about an upcoming vacation, for example. At the next level, hope is an acquired, *natural virtue*, providing the force to get something done. The natural virtue of hope involves the movement of both the emotions and the will. It pushes us to act, to move forward, as we might be inspired to do when we land a great new job or start writing a senior thesis.

If we are in a state of grace, the natural virtue of hope may become an infused *moral virtue*—the next level. For example, we may hope to find a spouse, but only if it is the will of God. We may hope for something particular, but we accept divine providence, which is greater than our will. The moral virtue of hope is paradoxical in nature and can be quite a challenge to live out, since it suggests both an active orientation to achieve a goal and a passive and loving acceptance of God's plan for us, regardless of our goals. Jesus exemplifies this virtue in His prayer in the Garden of Gethsemane: "Father, if you are willing, take this cup away from me; still, not my will but yours be done" (Luke 22:42).

Finally, and at the highest level, there is the *theological virtue* of hope, infused in us at baptism by grace:

> It is located in human will, adapting human will to the mysterious plan of God as it unfolds in our lives. God is leading us and unfolding His divine mystery step by step. Through the virtue of hope, we want what God wants. Hope involves acceptance of the divine mystery as it unfolds in our lives. We grow in hope as we let go of attachments.[92]

When I was a young girl in the 1970s, my family lived close to Disneyland. This was before Disney World and before the inexhaustible array of children's entertainment options that exist today. Life did not get better than a day spent at Disneyland. I still remember the overpowering excitement I felt leading up to our trips to the Magic Kingdom. Reflecting on these memories suggested a metaphor that helps me understand the four different meanings of hope. Might the theological virtue of hope be likened to this joyful expectation of time spent at Disneyland? To flesh out this metaphor, let's imagine that my parents told us kids that on the way to Disneyland we would be making a stop at an ordinary playground. Eagerly anticipating the stop at the ordinary playground, with little regard for Disneyland, our ultimate destination, would be an expression of the *emotion* of hope. Lacing up our sneakers in the car in preparation of running around the playground reflects the *natural* virtue of hope. If, along the way, my parents decide to drive right past that ordinary playground, and we were to take it in stride—thinking, "That's okay. As much as I was looking forward to a fun little break along the route, I know something a whole lot better is coming"—that would be an exercise of the *moral virtue* of hope. On the other hand, pitching a fit in the back of the car when the eagerly anticipated pit stop did not happen would violate

[92] Fr. Wojciech Giertych, O.P., Women's retreat, Stamford, Connecticut, August 2016.

the moral virtue of hope, as would stewing and moaning about not getting what *we* wanted.

Squeezing a bit more out of the Disneyland metaphor, to this day I vividly remember how crestfallen I was when my mom canceled a planned trip to Disneyland while my grandmother was visiting. Why? My brother and I had misbehaved. (Or was it just me?) How many times we hear parents threatening action against their misbehaving children, never to follow through! Kids figure this out very quickly. They learn that words and threats are meaningless, and consequences are insignificant. No risk of that with my mother, however; she wouldn't budge — an early lesson in the existence of Hell, perhaps. Thanks to such lessons, to this day, I know in my gut that actions have consequences.

Christian hope is accompanied by fear of God — specifically, fear of offending God. The lack of holy fear easily leads to presumption, the certitude of salvation. And this, in turn, leads to sluggishness. The concern about disappointing God should not make us neurotic but, rather, should lead us to have a childlike trust in God and to take His guiding hand. It should encourage us to strive please God, trusting that He will provide all the grace we need to do so.

Just as we pray for an increase in faith and charity, we should pray that our hope, too, be increased and purified. This means accepting our weaknesses and the precariousness of our lives and placing our unbounded confidence in the love and faithfulness of God.

The disciples at Emmaus and the mother of the sons of Zebedee are two clear Gospel examples of hope needing purification. The disciples hoped in their own plan, rather than God's. As a result, their hope was shattered, since things didn't turn out as they expected. Their house, built on sand, collapsed with the unwanted, unanticipated Crucifixion. Jesus chastised the disciples, saying, "Oh, how foolish you are!" (Luke 24:25). Their hope had to be purified to accept a mystery much greater than their expectations. Those who are locked in their own ideas are foolish. Instead, we need to interpret everything in light of the eternal divine project of God, our Father. As we live out the virtue of hope, we touch God and please Him, as we do when we exercise faith.

Anyone living on the Upper West Side of Manhattan can fully appreciate the Jewish mother of the sons of Zebedee, who provides us with another example of hope in need of purification. This mother of the "sons of thunder" (Mark 3:17) approaches Jesus to ask that her sons be seated at His right and left hand in His Kingdom (Matt. 20:20–28). The lesson here is pretty obvious. Our hope should not reside in honors or esteem. Instead, we should pray that our hope, our desires, be purified.

Our hope should also be practical and concrete, focused on specific things—a Manhattan parking space, even—but always in view of God's will for us. I used to pray in very specific terms for a good husband. But, like the Emmaus disciples, it was my will that was front and center. Mine was not a hope rooted in the question "What do you want for me, God?"

I used to do a fair bit of horseback riding (inspiring the most frivolous purchase I ever made: a thoroughbred horse). On a riding vacation in Sligo, Ireland, the friend accompanying me was thrown off her horse during a high-speed gallop on the shores of a long beach "under bare Ben Bulben's head."[93]

After a second harrowing experience, dealing with Irish socialized health care, we learned that my friend had cracked a few vertebrae. No more riding "where Ben Bulben sets the scene"[94] for us. With my friend sprawled across the backseat, I established myself as captain of our new mode of transportation, a rented car, and led us on a tour of the backroads of Ireland. First stop:

[93] William Butler Yeats, "Under Ben Bulben," VI.

[94] Ibid., I.

the Marian Shrine of Knock. There I remember pleading with God that I might meet a man like St. Joseph. I also made sure to inform Him that I had made quite a sacrifice to get myself to that shrine.

Only gradually was my hope purified, and my pleas evolved into "Whatever Your will is, God." My prayers today are filled with heartfelt gratitude for His having patiently led me to Himself. THANK YOU, LORD! God's plan for me was greater than mine.

Contemplative Souls and Their Natural Gifts

> When these souls discover the great attraction of solitude with God, usually after some years of struggle, their hearts are finally at peace. The solitary heart becomes for them an enclosure for God, and they are at last content. They have found the inner sanctum where, alone with God, they are never really alone.[95]

Does God call souls already gifted with a contemplative nature to be dedicated singles? Or does the dedicated-single vocation provide the rich opportunity to receive contemplative graces?[96]

95 Haggerty, *Conversion*, 237.

96 "We are so blessed!" wrote my friend Susan Conroy. "We get to spend more time with God, Who is everything! When God is with you, you have EVERYTHING! As a single person, you get to swim in the vast ocean of God's Love, basking in His Presence every day.... So many who are married with children naturally have to rush off after Mass (after Holy Communion, this holy union with Our Lord), and their hearts are pulled in many directions, but we have this exquisite opportunity to give ourselves wholeheartedly to God and to stay with Him. It's off the charts beautiful! We've got the gold! It just has to be appreciated."

Either way, those who discern a call to the dedicated-single vocation and generously embrace this call as God's loving will for them are uniquely positioned to practice the dispositions leading to perfection: self-giving, humility, and interior silence. Three great masters of Carmelite spirituality—St. John of the Cross, St. Teresa of Avila, and St. Thérèse of Lisieux—emphasized these three foundational dispositions as vital for a soul's ultimate perfection.[97]

I used to think I was afforded the opportunity to learn Spanish because of my career choice, as I spent much of my time working in Latin America. When I read St. John of the Cross's poem "The Spiritual Canticle," the thought occurred to me that this may be the true reason I learned Spanish—God wanted me to read this poem. St. Pope John Paul II studied Spanish later in life so that he could read John of the Cross's writings in the original language. I understand why. "The Spiritual Canticle" is a passionate love story between God and His beloved, inspired by imagery from the Song of Songs. The poem's forty stanzas powerfully express, as best as I've ever known mere words to convey, the various stages and layers of a love affair between God and His chosen beloved, each of us. In stanza 35 of the second redaction, St. John captures exquisitely the solitary nature of the dedicated-single vocation:

> En soledad vivía,
> y en soledad ha puesto ya su nido,
> y en soledad la guía
> a solas su querido
> también en soledad de amor herido
>
> She lived in solitude,
> and now in solitude has built her nest;

[97] P. Marie-Eugene de l'Enfant Jesus, O.C.D., *I Want to See God* (Philippines: Society of St. Paul, 2007), 362.

and in solitude he guides her,
he alone, who also bears
in solitude the wound of love.[98]

On the literal level, the repetition of the word "solitude" makes an obvious reference to the fact that most dedicated lay singles live alone. But solitude is not loneliness. Indeed, human companionship can cause loneliness. No human companionship can fill the heart of one who longs for God.

Developing and sustaining a relationship with God requires solitude and silence so that we may gaze upon Him, speak to Him, listen to Him—so that we can properly pray. Our world has become noisy and our lives frenetic. God speaks in whispers. Overly busy, media-obsessed lives lived alone are not lives of solitude. The life of solitude that St. John writes about is one in which the soul makes room for God, allowing Him to build a "nest" so that the soul can find rest and comfort.

It took me many years to realize that I did not have to go out and socialize anytime I was asked, nor was I obliged to do the asking. The more time I spend in solitude, the more I can be who God wants me to be amid the bustle. I think the majority of those God calls to be His alone in the world are introverted by nature, drawing energy from solitude.

But unlike the cloistered nun or monk, the dedicated single is called to leaven the world from within, in the messy thick of things. The dedicated single is a complex combination of the contemplative and the messy incarnational expression of faith in the world. As much as contemplative-oriented dedicated singles yearn to

[98] St. John of the Cross, "The Spiritual Canticle," in *The Collected Works of St. John of the Cross*, trans. Kieran Kavanaugh, O.C.D., and Otilio Rodriguez, O.C.D. (Washington, D.C.: Institute of Carmelite Studies, 1991), 79.

nestle in solitude in the finely woven nests of their souls, where God resides, they are called to go forth. This idea of the go-forth calling brings to mind two Gospel moments: the Transfiguration and Mary Magdalene's interaction with Christ after the Resurrection. At the Transfiguration, the three chosen disciples want to erect tents and hang out forever with Jesus after His divinity is revealed to them at the top of Mount Tabor. Mary Magdalene, too, wants to keep the resurrected Jesus tightly in her grasp. On both occasions Jesus ends the party early, ordering the disciples to descend the mountain and Mary Magdalene to let go of Him. After experiencing the loving embrace of God, we are called to bring a taste of this paradise to others.

From the protected, beautifully tended nest in the soul, God alone guides His dedicated single. Unlike spouses and religious, who live more outwardly structured lives that progress along a path carved out by family demands or obedience to a superior, ours is not a clear-cut path. A single laywoman in early twentieth-century France, Venerable Madeleine Delbrêl, in her poem, "Launching Ourselves Forward in Love" describes it this way: "You refuse to give us a road map. Our journey takes place at night." An externally circumscribed state of life does not illuminate our daily pathway. God does so quietly but assuredly, through the maternal guidance of His visible Church and through the divinely ordained circumstances and encounters of our daily lives.

Discerning what I believe to be God's will has typically come easily for me, that is, if one considers spending time on one's knees easy. God provides more consolations and speaks a bit louder to dedicated singles, I think, as we normally do not have immediate and clearly delineated family obligations or the structure of religious life to guide our days. Good spiritual reading, too, is critical to discernment. I cannot count how many times my daily spiritual reading reveals a point that is pertinent to what I am grappling with at the moment.

I've come to realize that this spiritual reading is an important avenue by which the Holy Spirit provides specific guidance.

As a voracious yet discerning reader, I receive most of my spiritual insights from Sacred Scripture, particularly as it is presented through the liturgical cycle, and from the spiritual masters. For doctrinal insight, papal documents are an underappreciated spiritual resource. Frankly, there is a lot of pablum out there. It makes no sense to imbibe bland or poisonous mush when the Catholic Church makes available a delectable feast of spiritual readings. When, in response to my request for suggested spiritual reading, my spiritual director responded, "You seem to have identified them well enough on your own," I realized the Holy Spirit had long been directing my reading choices.

Our paths are forged, first and foremost, by taking the hand of Jesus and being attentive to His unique design for us, as we do not receive much guiding light from human models. Jesus is the perfect model for dedicated singles. He lived in perfect obedience to the will of His Father, discerned through constant prayer.

Beyond the physical solitude evoked throughout "The Spiritual Canticle," especially in the thirty-fifth stanza, St. John of the Cross also expresses metaphorically the essence of spiritual solitude: a heightened spiritual state of compete detachment from earthly things and people—poverty of spirit, forged in purifying, painful fires. Those whose hearts are freed from earthly attachments, desires, expectations, and self-will are more receptive to the lavish reward of perfect love that only God can bestow. God wants to shower us with His love and grace, but we have to let Him.

The Lord, "who also bears in solitude the wound of love," makes Himself vulnerable to our response. "[God's] eyes linger on certain souls, watching them for a time, before targeting them as a prey of His love."[99] God is a gentleman and will not force Himself on

[99] Haggerty, *Conversion*, 24.

us. Even more, He makes Himself vulnerable to us. He is touched by our love for Him, especially if it is singularly focused on Him. Though persistent, He will give us only as much as we allow. We need to do our part to help Him remove the obstacles in our hearts. And sometimes the little obstacles, the tiny dust balls lurking in the corners of our hearts, are harder to remove than the big pieces of furniture that fill our hearts at the beginning of God's courtship with us. A thin thread of attachment prevents a bird from flight just as effectively as a thick rope, St. John of the Cross warns.

St. Thérèse of Lisieux was graced with an extraordinarily personalized faith. So confident was she of God's particular love for her that she audaciously offered herself up to the Infant Jesus as a child's toy for His amusement. She knew that she could be a source of joy for God, a means to make Jesus smile, if not laugh.

I think that those with deep prayer lives conceive of their relationship with God in countless ways, depending on their personalities, experiences, and the particular circumstances of the moment. Many prayerful souls imagine their relationship with God either as one of their consoling Him, perhaps at the foot of the Cross, or of God consoling them, like a parent consoling a little child or an infant.

Chapter 8

Consecration, Vows, and Dedicated Singles

We are all aware of the treasure which the gift of the consecrated life in the variety of its charisms and institutions represents for the ecclesial community. Together let us thank God for the religious orders and institutes devoted to contemplation or the works of the apostolate, for societies of apostolic life, for secular institutes, and for other groups of consecrated persons, as well as for all those individuals who, in their inmost hearts, dedicate themselves to God by a special consecration.

—Pope John Paul II, *Vita Consecrata*, no. 2

An important lesson I learned in my search to understand where a dedicated single person fits into the Church is that one mustn't lose the forest for the trees—that is, it is crucial not to fixate on vows and religious categories at the expense of knowing and loving God. It is helpful, however, to develop a clear understanding of the distinct states of life and vocations that are recognized by the Church to support the full expression of one's baptismal promises.

For a long time, it was commonly held that to be a saint, one had to be a religious. Vatican II helped to correct this misperception, emphasizing the unchanging tenet of our Faith that baptism provides all the graces necessary to become a saint in any state of life. For those who truly desire holiness, what is most important is living out the theological virtues: faith, hope, and charity. How the theological virtues are expressed through one's daily life, which is informed by one's state in life and particular vocation, is more important than whether one professes religious vows or is ordained. Christ is made present in the world through the generous exercising of our unique gifts in the particular circumstances God has designed for each of us.

The questions I had concerning vows and consecrated life in the Church were answered by careful reading of both the *Code of Canon Law* and *Christian Totality: Theology of the Consecrated Life*,[100] as well as through conversations with a few patient canon lawyers.

Dedicated singles are not consecrated in the Church's eyes, contrary to what some think, nor are they just like nuns or monks living out in the world. This is not to say that, in the lived expressions of the various states of life or vocations, lines have not been blurred. Some religious act as lay "wannabees," and some laypersons act as religious "wannabees."

All baptized Christians are consecrated, since baptism incorporates us into God's family as His adopted children and into His Mystical Body, the Church. This makes us sacred. Jesus is the Bridegroom of the Church and of each faithful soul. In addition to our baptismal vows, most of us take civil oaths or make secular pledges of one sort or another during our lives—saying the Pledge of Allegiance or taking an oath, hand on Bible, in a court of law, and so forth.

In Church parlance, however, clearly defined in the *Code of Canon Law*, vows and consecration have more specific meanings beyond baptismal and civil pledges. Canon law gets a bad rap these days. It is sometimes perceived as overly complicated or even

[100] Basil Cole, O.P., and Paul Conner, O.P., *Christian Totality: Theology of the Consecrated Life* (New York: Alba House, 1997).

pharisaical. On the contrary, it is quite accessible and readable, and more importantly, it defines how the Church governs herself so that she can most efficaciously lead souls to Heaven. The Church is concerned about spiritual realities as they are lived out in the material world, and this requires clearly defined rules and norms.

To be consecrated within the Church means to give oneself to God in a more radical way than stipulated by baptism. This is done by professing vows to follow permanently the three evangelical counsels of obedience, poverty, and chastity, which are meant to bolster the three theological virtues. Whereas baptismal consecration rejects the evil works of Satan, consecration vows to set aside good things—autonomy, possessions, and marriage—for the love of Christ, establishing a spousal relationship with Him.

Being consecrated does not necessarily equate to being a religious, that is, a nun, sister, monk, or friar, though the majority of consecrated souls are religious. But the consecrated life is a broader category, encompassing various canonically approved ways of living out the evangelical counsels in a stable, structured way, either as a hermit, an anchorite, a consecrated virgin, or a consecrated layperson.

As defined by canon law, there are two broad avenues of living as a consecrated person. These include living as a member of a *society of apostolic life* or as a member of an *institute of consecrated life*. Members of societies of apostolic life live out the evangelical counsels without taking public vows.[101] Rather, they make a

[101] The *Code of Canon Law* (can. 731) describes societies of apostolic life as resembling "institutes of consecrated life; their members, without religious vows, pursue the apostolic purpose proper to the society and, leading a life in common as brothers or sisters according to their proper manner of life, strive for the perfection of charity through the observance of the constitutions." Members of societies of apostolic life do not make public vows but, rather,

commitment to live out the evangelical counsels as members of an apostolic society, and this commitment establishes an officially recognized "sacred bond."

Under the category of institutes of consecrated life, there are two types of institutes: *secular institutes* and *institutes of religious life*. Members of secular institutes also do not normally profess vows, though they may. Instead, they normally make *sacred promises* to live out the evangelical counsels in the world as institute members.[102] Members of institutes of religious life necessarily *do* make public vows, committing themselves to live apart from the world:

> [Religious] live out the three vows publicly within a legal structure that has its rule, religious habit, and specific customs. Thus, they are a "state," distinct from the laity. They live in their communities, obey superiors, follow their rule. The try to live out the contemplative life of faith, hope, and

---

a *commitment* to live out the evangelical counsels. Accordingly, they are technically not religious in the canonical sense. They are consecrated though, a distinction recognized by few, even by Catholics, themselves, and understandably so.

[102] The *Code of Canon Law* (can. 710) defines *secular institute* as "an institute of consecrated life in which the Christian faithful, living in the world, strive for the perfection of charity and seek to contribute to the sanctification of the world, especially from within." Secular institute members normally do not profess public vows but, rather, *sacred promises*. Like members of societies of apostolic life, canon law recognizes secular institute members as consecrated but not as religious.

Secular Institutes were formally recognized by Pope Pius XII in the apostolic constitution, *Provida Mater Ecclesia*, published February 2, 1947. Pius XII also published an anniversary *motu proprio*, *Primo Feliciter*, on March 12, 1948. Both these documents are well worth a read for an understanding of the charism and history of secular institutes and to gain an appreciation for how the Church responds to creative and new inspirations from the Holy Spirit.

> charity, strengthened by the vows of poverty, chastity, and obedience, within the religious structure of their order. They touch the world with the richness of their contemplative life from without, from their religious community, monastery, the visible and legal structure that sets them "apart from the world." The structure of the "state of the religious life" offers protection to the contemplative life, with its rules, theological tradition, community life, and spirituality.[103]

According to canon law, only members of institutes of religious life are technically *religious*, though many of us do not make such ecclesial distinctions and think of all consecrated as "religious."

The Church is a master at balancing paradox. Christianity, itself, is one big paradox. God subjected His Son to human degradation and "failure" as the means to redeem all humanity. Holy Scripture exhorts us to follow the Ten Commandments, yet one of our greatest saints, Augustine, advises us simply to "love and do what you will." In Matthew 5:48, we are exhorted to "be perfect as our heavenly Father is perfect," yet in many other Gospel passages, we are told that we are unworthy sinners. God is limitless, yet He works in a special way within circumscribed rubrics of the sacraments. The Holy Spirit has inspired the Church to recognize canonically three distinct states of life, yet myriad Church-recognized ways of living out one's vocation have emerged over the centuries combining various features of all three states of life. In this way, a certain degree of rigidity *and* flexibility characterizes the Church's response to the Holy Spirit's creative work in her members at various moments in history.

Active religious orders, such as the Dominicans and the Franciscans, as opposed to contemplative orders, such as the Benedictines

[103] Wojciech Giertych, O.P., private e-mail.

and the Carmelites, first emerged during the Middle Ages in response to the great need for public evangelizers. These active orders have been operating outside of monastery walls for centuries.

Societies of apostolic life—such as the Daughters of Charity of St. Vincent de Paul, Maryknoll, the Pallottines, and the Paulist Fathers—emerged in the eighteenth and nineteenth centuries in response to the needs of a rapidly changing society for an even greater apostolic, social thrust. Despite being active in the world outside the confines of monastery walls, these active religious orders and societies of apostolic life retained a strong sense of separation from the world, living structured, regulated, communal lives and wearing distinctive habits—that is, until the later part of the twentieth century.

The more recent emergence of secular institutes in the twentieth century—such as Caritas Christi, Notre-Dame de Vie, and the Schoenstatt Movement—is an exciting, important, and underappreciated development in the Church. Secular institutes unite the extremes of Christian life within the Church: contemplation and action, hiddenness and public witness, in the world and apart from the world. Secular-institute members live in the lay state but are also consecrated, having committed themselves to the evangelical counsels, and may correctly wear the label "consecrated laity."[104] They are called to direct their external apostolic zeal, nourished by interior contemplation, into the world by living very much in the world. They are not simply a new form of traditional religious order; they are something altogether new but with roots that go far back in history.

[104] Dedicated singles and Opus Dei numeraries who are lay celibates are sometimes mistakenly referred to as consecrated laity. Since they do not ecclesiastically commit themselves to the three evangelical counsels, they are not publicly or formally consecrated in the eyes of the Church.

According to the "founding document" of secular institutes for the consecrated lay state, *Provida Mater Ecclesia*:

> Not only do [secular-institute members] strive for personal perfection: they remain in the world, thanks to a special divine vocation, and have discovered excellent new forms of association that correspond best to modern demands, in which they can lead a life that is extremely well suited to the attaining of Christian perfection.[105]

Secular-institute members are consecrated in exactly the same way as religious, but they are not in the religious state. They are fully consecrated, taking vows of perpetual poverty, chastity, and obedience, but they do so as laity. They touch the world with the richness of their contemplative life from within, being present but hidden in the world.

Members of secular institutes may or may not live in community, and their charism is very much oriented outward, toward the world. They typically have secular careers, and, based on exterior appearances, they may look no different from other laypersons. I say, "may," because they are called to dress modestly, which, given the risqué bent of fashion these days, sometimes makes them stand out starkly. In such cases, they may deservedly be praised for "wearing their dogma loudly."

I think of the dedicated-single vocation as a hybrid of the newly defined secular institutes and of the age-old consecrated virgins, whose roots go back to the earliest days of the Church. Like secular-institute members, dedicated singles are exclusively and permanently committed to Christ and also totally present in today's world. Both make a vow or promise of celibacy and lead lives that balance action and contemplation. But unlike secular-institute members,

[105] *Provida Mater Ecclesia*, no. 7.

who make vows of material poverty and obedience, dedicated singles strive to embrace the spirit of these evangelical counsels, rather than their material fulfillment. Moreover, dedicated singles do not undergo official formation or an externally defined spiritual program, nor do they have a structured community. Dedicated singles are like consecrated virgins, on the other hand, in that they are called to a deeply spousal relationship with Christ.

This unique calling to be brides of Christ is explicitly confirmed by the Church in the consecration of virgins. Canon 604 §1 describes consecrated virgins:

> Similar to these forms of consecrated life is the order of virgins who, expressing the holy resolution of following Christ more closely, are consecrated to God by the diocesan bishop according to the approved liturgical rite, are mystically betrothed to Christ, the Son of God, and are dedicated to the service of the Church.

A consecrated virgin's spousal relationship with Christ is the cornerstone of this long-storied vocation in the Church. Consecrated virgins were a major spiritual force during the early, persecution-laden centuries of the Church and were precursors to the nuns of the first religious orders that emerged in the Middle Ages. Their numbers and visibility in the Church waned with the emergence of myriad religious institutes over the centuries. Then, in 1927, the Congregation for Religious officially suppressed the use of the *Rite of Consecration to a Life of Virginity* for women living "in the world." Decades later, as part of Vatican II's focus on the Church Fathers and early life of the Church as a source of renewal for the modern age, a renewed appreciation for the unique charism of consecrated virginity developed. The 1970 publication of the revised *Rite of Consecration to a Life of Virginity* brought this vocation back to the Church, and the 1983 *Code of Canon Law* formally recognized the reestablishment of consecrated virginity as a distinct category of consecrated life.

Like consecrated virgins, dedicated singles I know experience a very personal, spousal relationship with Christ, whether or not they explicitly acknowledge or are able to articulate this important component of their vocation. While bridal imagery and language is an element of some religious charisms, it is not usually the main focus. A more generalized orientation toward the profession of vows and toward apostolic service tends to receive greater emphasis than the one-on-one, intimate spousal relationship with Christ.

The best resource I've come across for understanding both the consecrated vocation and the dedicated-single vocation is the *Sponsa-Christi* blog, written by a very thoughtful, bright consecrated virgin who has advanced degrees in theology and canon law. According to the blog, what makes a dedicated single intensely different from a consecrated virgin is the very private nature of the dedicated-single vocation. A consecrated virgin is consecrated in the Church as part of the public prayer of the Church. As the *Sponsa-Christi* blogger writes, "Her vocation doesn't 'belong' to her as much as it belongs to the entire people of God." In a wonderfully illustrative and creative comparison, the blogger associates consecrated virgins with the public prayer of the Church — the Mass and the Liturgy of the Hours — whereas dedicated singles are associated with the private, often contemplative, prayer of its individual members. (See the appendix about discerning a call to dedicated-single life versus consecrated virginity).

Vows

As it relates to understanding where dedicated singles fit into the Church, clarity about the Church's understanding of vows is important. Many dedicated singles I know grapple with the question of whether they should take vows. The priests to whom I've posed the question have taken a cautious stance, understandably. Vows are weighty obligations. And there are serious consequences to breaking vows with respect to our relationship with God. Vows are to be taken very seriously, with thoughtful discernment and, preferably, with the accompaniment of a spiritual director.

Vows are specific acts of worship that have a sacred character and are governed by canon law. According to canon 1191 §1, "A vow, that is, a deliberate and free promise made to God about a possible and better good, must be fulfilled by reason of the virtue of religion." Canon law outlines various classifications of vows—such as temporary versus perpetual, public versus private, solemn versus simple, personal versus real—and under what circumstances and by whom a vow can be dispensed.

There is precious little formal guidance written concerning the conditions or circumstances under which a dedicated single should take vows and what exactly the form of such vows might be. Indeed, there is a great deal of flexibility with respect to the manner in which private vows are made and to their content. Dedicated singles I know who have taken private vows have all written their vows themselves.

What canon law does explicitly state is that dedicated singles are allowed to take simple but not solemn vows, and private but not public vows. Simple vows allow ownership of property, whereas solemn vows do not. Solemn vows are perpetual, and they make contrary acts, such as getting married, not only illicit but also invalid. The difference between simple and solemn vows gets at the heart of the difference between nuns and sisters. Nuns profess solemn vows, while sisters profess simple perpetual vows. The difference between private and public vows is stipulated in canon 1192 §2: "A vow is public if a legitimate superior accepts it in the name of the Church; otherwise it is private." Dedicated singles can take both temporary vows, which are typically renewed, or perpetual vows. It is recommended that one first profess temporary vows before ultimately professing perpetual vows.

Vows are a manifestation of the virtue of religion, an often-overlooked moral virtue. Tied to the virtue of justice, the virtue of religion pertains to the way we render to God what is His due. The Ten Commandments concretely outline the minimum way in which we are called to render to God His due, and they also serve as a road map for our peace and joy. Vows or sacred promises commit one to make an even greater gift to God than one's baptismal promises. Professing vows or sacred promises means doing something more for God in concrete terms.

Of the three evangelical counsels, perfect chastity is the one private vow that a layperson, whether affiliated with a secular institute or not, can objectively make. A dedicated single can, through careful discernment, decide to give herself or himself to Christ, permanently renouncing marriage, with no formal permission from others. This is an extraordinary gift to make and one that entails a richness of meaning on both the temporal and spiritual planes. Renouncing marriage for love of God is a true vocation. Making a private vow of chastity in the face of the Church, witnessed by a spiritual director or a confessor, helps one to persevere in this vocation.

As for the evangelical counsel of obedience, a dedicated single, unassociated with a canonically approved institute, is not in a position to vow objective obedience to someone, even to a spiritual director, in the same way as the religious or consecrated do. Moreover, single laypersons must manage their own finances and prudently plan for their old age, as they are not financially taken care of by a Church community. Accordingly, they cannot, or should not, vow objective poverty.

What dedicated singles can vow, in addition to chastity, are positive things, such as prayer commitments, acts of charity, sacrifices, or fasting. These are tangible, measurable acts that express one's love for God, similar to the vows taken in marriage, in which couples promise certain acts to one another (to be there in sickness and health, to love and honor each other, and so forth). Prayer commitments might be thought of as a formal promise to communicate regularly and lovingly with one's heavenly Spouse, and acts of charity or sacrifices might be thought of as tangible ways of expressing one's love.

The very holy friend I have mentioned previously has taken private vows of chastity in the presence of a priest. I wrote to her at the time, saying, "This is more about a step forward than an entry into something completely different because you and I have been externally living this life for a while already. The change (profound still) will be internal." While it was not an entry into something different, it certainly proved to be an entry into a state of great joy and peace. My friend has been beaming ever since making her private vows to Jesus, and it has been nearly two years now.

A Hidden Vocation in Uncertain Times

Some bemoan what they perceive to be a diminished distinction between the religious and lay states. To what degree this concern is warranted is not easy to determine. It ties in with a broader, complex story, whose basic backdrop is important for understanding the dedicated-single vocation today.

Never in the history of mankind has society experienced such a rapid pace of change as it has over the past century. Change in the social and moral realms picked up steam during the revolutionary, "rule-breaking" 1960s, when the Second Vatican Council was held. The goal of Vatican II was to let some air into the Church in order to better evangelize and spiritually feed a radically changing world. But does opening up to the world mean embracing its secular values? Battles over this question have been quietly and not so quietly fought since Vatican II. Indeed, the recent uproar over Pope Francis's *Amoris Laetitia* reflects conflicting views as to where this line should be drawn between the world's values and how the Church upholds the Word of God.

More than a few priests and religious from traditional religious orders interpreted Vatican II as license to engage the world in a manner very different from that envisioned by their founders or by Church tradition. Rules regulating community and prayer life were relaxed, street clothes replaced habits and clerical clothing, and many left the religious and ordained states altogether. In some instances, the authentic charisms of traditional orders were abandoned, and liturgical beauty and reverence was replaced by informality, banality, and downright ugliness. Among the bitter fruits has been the drastic decrease of female religious in the United States, from 180,000 in 1965 to 47,000 today, and a steep decline in priests from 58,000 to 37,000 during the same period.[106]

Since Vatican II, the laity has played a growing role in the Church (though limited in terms of institutional responsibility). In one obvious respect, this has been a healthy evolution, as it has encouraged the laity to cultivate their faith lives more actively. The resurgence of lay movements, such as Communion and Liberation and Focolare, reflects one avenue by which many laypersons have responded to a desire for greater faith formation, community, and apostolic structure imbued with a particular charism.

Since Vatican II, firmly fixed lines between the states of life have softened. Roles historically limited to clergy or consecrated persons are now being played by the laity, and vice versa. Are "rigidly" circumscribed roles in the Church anachronistic in today's

[106] Center for Applied Research in the Apostolate (CARA), "Frequently Requested Church Statistics," https://cara.georgetown.edu/frequently-requested-church-statistics/.

more fluid society? Or are highly delineated, distinct, divinely inspired roles serving an important temporal function in the life of the Church? Some think that women should be allowed to be ordained, and others think it is unseemly for women theologians to teach at seminaries. It seems that society has become too fluid, unstable, bereft of a humanizing social scaffolding that, for millennia, supported individuals in tight-knit communities. So how ought the Church to respond? How can the Church remain a stable anchor against the powerful tides of sociological change, not to mention the rapidly changing moral landscape?

It is against this complex backdrop that the number of dedicated-single vocations has grown, in tandem with consecrated lay vocations. More are being called to live out their baptismal vows in creative, hybrid ways. These are high-risk, high-reward vocations. Secular-institute members must have strong spiritual lives because they do not have the protection of the visible structure of the religious state. Dedicated singles are even more "on their own."

By their very nature, these are hidden, under-the-radar vocations. As Fr. Carleton Jones, O.P., beautifully expressed to me, "Your vowed status is hidden; people come to know it once they come to know you; they detect a difference." If lived well, these vocations represent little lights in an increasingly dark world. If nourished properly, they can also be extraordinarily fruitful vocations. But too few in the Church know about, understand, or see value in these hidden vocations. How many souls whom Christ is calling to be His alone in the world do not respond to His call only because they do not know that this special vocation is even a possibility?

Chapter 9

Dedicated Singles and the Evangelical Counsels

Perfection consists in the observance of the counsels, all of which, like the commandments, are directed to charity; yet not in the same way. For the commandments, other than the precepts of charity, are directed to the removal of things contrary to charity, with which, namely, charity is incompatible, whereas the counsels are directed to the removal of things that hinder the act of charity, and yet are not contrary to charity, such as marriage, the occupation of worldly business, and so forth. . . . Hence it is that in the Conferences of the Fathers (Coll. I, cap. vii) the abbot Moses says: 'Fastings, watchings, meditating on the Scriptures, penury, and loss of all one's wealth, these are not perfection but means to perfection, since not in them does the school of perfection find its end, but through them it achieves its end.' "

—Thomas Aquinas, *Summa Theologiae*, II-II, q. 184, art. 3

The "spirit" of the evangelical counsels is quite simply the spirit of the Church."

—Hans Urs von Balthasar, *The Laity and the Life of the Counsels*

The evangelical counsels—chastity, poverty, and obedience—are a helpful *means to an end*, that end being perfect charity. Perfect charity is union with God, and it is reached when one gives one's whole life back to God. The counsels are a concrete means of expressing total, unconditional availability. For those called to live by them, the counsels can serve as an express train to perfect charity.

Objectively living out the counsels entails firm obedience to a superior, and this is possible only in a stable, long-term community. It requires a rule and a structure, and this is not something that can be invisible. A state of life in the Church should be visible, not hidden. A dedicated single is not a secret or hidden religious, but a layperson. One can objectively vow perfect chastity for the rest of one's life while immersed in the world. But, as mentioned earlier, it is extremely difficult and not advisable for those living alone in the world to take vows of objective poverty and obedience. In contrast, members of secular institutes, who are lay and who often work in secular settings, have the support of a community that does enable them to take objective vows of poverty and obedience.

To some degree, we are all called to live a *spirit* of poverty and obedience and to be chaste according to our states in life. Indeed, St. Paul exhorts, "From now on, let those having wives act as not having them ... those buying as not owning, those using the world as not using it fully" (1 Cor. 7:29–31). The secular world is in great need of sanctification:

> There is today no more direct way to bear holiness into the spheres and the professional jobs of the laity than this combination of the lay state with the state of the counsels.... It is the way to establish the pure Christian type of professional work for the most diverse lay professions.[107]

The secular institutes represent one form of synthesis between the lay state and the state of the counsels. Might there be room

[107] Hans Urs von Balthasar, *The Laity and the Life of the Counsels: The Church's Mission in the World* (San Francisco: Ignatius Press, 2003), Kindle Cloud, loc. 996.

for another type of synthesis—dedicated singles living out the counsels in a modified way? The evangelical counsels lived even in an objective spiritual hybrid can claim everything for love of God—comfort, will, and heart. The heart is most important, and it is what we give to God when we make a vow of perfect chastity. Perfect chastity, or celibacy, has the richest spiritual meaning of the counsels.

Dedicated singles, along with secular-institute members, serve another important function apart from being a powerful leaven in secular society. Compared with most clergy and religious, those who excel in professional fields are better equipped with knowledge, experience, and time to address the pressing moral issues of the day, those involving technology, health, finance, and the environment. In a hard-hitting critique, Balthasar writes:

> Within the Orders that exist today, with the exception of certain school congregations, there is no longer any place for an educated layman.... It is practically impossible today to lead the life of the evangelical counsels as a doctor, lawyer, politician, journalist, and so on, in secular positions, since only the theologian is permitted to combine the life of the counsels with a professional course of study. The first effect of this is apathy, which is difficult to put one's finger on but undeniably present, on the part of the educated laity not only vis-à-vis the state of the counsels, but also vis-à-vis the pronouncements that the hierarchy make about the professional fields of the laity.... The gap between the specialized professional ... and the specialized theologian ... has become too great to permit a calm discussion of professional questions.[108]

[108] Balthasar, *The Laity.*, loc. 928.

Balthasar suggests that we look to a colorful, if not underappreciated, chapter in Church history for a model of how vowed laity could again play a more prominent role in the Church and society at large. The knightly orders were established to engage the world in a variety of ways, such as to conquer or defend the Holy Land, serve the poor, liberate Christian slaves, engage in commerce, and administer educational and legal systems. These early orders—such as the Marian knights of the Teutonic Order, the Order of Saint John, the Mercedarians, the Knights of Malta, and the Knights of the Holy Sepulchre—integrated the state of the evangelical counsels with secular activity, proving the ideal that secular activity could be sanctified and perfected.

> When we look at the Orders that emerged in the Middle Ages, what surprises us is not so much the number of those who entered the state of the counsels as the almost unlimited imagination of the Christian soul, which effortlessly devised ever new ways of embodying perfect love as Christ commanded it and living them out in a naively realistic form that was at one and the same time literal and sublimely heroic. [109]

A historical model that Balthasar does *not* think is worth emulating is membership in what are called third orders. Third orders developed as a sort of lay concentric circle around the traditional and mendicant religious orders, such as the Carmelites, Dominicans, and Franciscans—the first order being the male religious, the second order referring to the cloistered nuns affiliated with the mendicant orders, and the third order comprising tertiaries, lay followers who spread the spirit of the order into the secular world. Balthasar highlights an inherent weakness in the third orders:

[109] Ibid., loc. 800 out of 3427.

> Since they lack that act of "leaving all things" in a total following of Christ that constitutes the state of life and is the unity that gives form to all the deeds and practices making up the life of the counsels, the rules for tertiaries ... must necessarily fall apart into a certain multiplicity of regulations.[110]

Going further, the tertiary mentality can fall prey to the mistaken notion that if you want to be a saint, you have to be a religious. It erroneously suggests that lay people have to follow religious rules and monastic observances—Balthasar's "multiplicity of regulations"—and tries to make quasi-religious out of laypeople.

Exploring various lived expressions of consecrated and lay life throughout Church history provides guiding lights for the exploration of new ways to live out the lay vocation in today's world. It is a fascinating topic and one that deserves more exploration. What I think is important to consider, as it relates to understanding the dedicated single vocation, is that the Holy Spirit has inspired many creative ways of responding to God's call over the centuries, and this should shape how Catholics think about vocational possibilities today. A deep understanding of the important differences between the religious and lay states is critical to forging a fruitful consecrated lay or dedicated-single vocation, which blends certain elements of these two states of life. Vocations in the secular world should not depend on a multiplicity of practices and prescriptions, which are specific to a traditional religious vocation.

Obedience

"Our Lord spent three hours in redeeming, three years in teaching, and thirty years in obeying, in order that a rebellious, proud,

[110] Balthasar, *The Laity*, loc. 888.

and diabolically independent world might learn the value of obedience," wrote Venerable Archbishop Fulton J. Sheen. "No heavenly call is ever to be trusted that bids one neglect the obvious duties that lie near to hand."[111]

Living the spirit of obedience well is most difficult for a dedicated single. The very attributes that make one suited to this vocation — independent-mindedness, creativity, courage — also feed a rebellious spirit.

Jesus provides the ultimate model of obedience. In obedience, Jesus expressed His dignity and His limitless sovereignty. How extraordinary that the young Jesus Christ, being both man and God, obeyed what God created, Mary and Joseph (see Luke 2:51). Disobedience caused our great fall, but the obedience of Mary and Jesus brought about our redemption.

Obedience is one of the highest expressions that love can take. It is listening to another and doing the other's will. How do children please their parents? They obey. How do married couples show their love for one another? They cede to the wishes of the other. How do we, as adopted children of our loving Father, show our gratitude? We submit to His loving plan for us, confident that *His* plan, not ours, is perfect.

Obedience has fallen out of favor in our culture. It is the most difficult evangelical council for many religious to follow. It is challenging because there is no better hammer than obedience to beat down that most insidious, hard-to-eradicate sin, pride. As mentioned earlier, obedience is a special challenge for dedicated singles owing to the vocation's inherent lack of structure and lack of earthly accountability as compared with religious, ordained, or married vocations. Dedicated singles create their own structure.

[111] Fulton J. Sheen, *The World's First Love* (San Francisco: Ignatius Press, 2010), 100, 101.

Even those blessed with a good spiritual director are not normally held accountable in the circumscribed manner that religious or even married are.

A dedicated single's secular profession, apostolic commitments, family, and friends provide the earthly "rules" to which a dedicated single is obedient. A spirit of obedience, a well-formed conscience, and Christ's promptings during prayer or through tangible daily events provide the spiritual means by which a layperson is obedient.

Discerning the promptings of the Lord requires much prayer and inner quiet, as, unlike most human spouses, our Spouse, Jesus, speaks to us ever so softly. Silence, whether exterior or interior, is a rare commodity these days. Cardinal Sarah beautifully expresses the importance of silence for the discernment of God's revealed will in his book *The Power of Silence: Against the Dictatorship of Noise*. Fostering an environment of silence at home generally is more attainable for a dedicated single than it is for others. This is an extraordinary privilege.

In addition to the need for silence, dedicated singles must also be self-disciplined, like children who do their homework without having to be asked by their parents. Religious who live in community are awakened early to attend morning prayers and Mass. Rolling over at the sound of the alarm to steal an extra hour of sleep instead of rising for prayer would be noticed and frowned on in a community. Similarly, rolling over at the sound of a child's screaming pleas just isn't an option. But for a dedicated single, no one would notice a decision to sleep in, except, perhaps, the handful of early-morning regulars at the 7:00 a.m. Mass.

The virtue of prudence powerfully aids in the practice of obedience. Although prudence sometimes gets a bad rap, being incorrectly perceived as uncourageous caution, it is the practical virtue of knowing how to act rightly. It is knowing how to navigate well the events of one's daily life, how to make sage decisions in the face of uncertainty. The virtues, especially prudence, enable us to carry out inspirations from the Holy Spirit actively, effectively, and obediently.

What can we do to react more prudently and obediently to the promptings of the Holy Spirit? First, we should be sure to receive the sacrament of confirmation. Our confirmation deepens our baptismal grace and increases in us the gifts of the Holy Spirit — wisdom, understanding, counsel, knowledge, piety, fortitude, and fear of the Lord. These gifts are like antennae, permanent structures in the soul that capture the divine radio waves emanating from a heavenly broadcaster, as Fr. Giertych puts it.

Our role is to open ourselves up so that our capacity for receiving these divine waves is increased. We want to make our receptive radio tower bigger and better through frequent prayer. Through prayer we exercise the theological virtues of faith, hope, and charity, which activate the gifts of the Holy Spirit, the antennae. We enter the supernatural realm when we pray. By exercising faith in prayer, we can touch God and activate a connection with Him.

We must also cultivate the virtues, especially the cardinal virtues of prudence, justice, fortitude, and temperance. This involves exercising our will; we must not, however, think we can develop the virtues through sheer willpower at the expense of prayer. Prayer is like turning over the keys of the car to God and asking Him to do the driving. This can be difficult for us Americans, who tend to want to do most of the driving ourselves.

A while back, a dear friend texted me to ask whether I was planning to attend a particular Mass in Portland, Maine. I had planned to attend a different Mass, which I preferred, but it also struck me that she wanted to connect for some reason. I was about to text that I would not be at "her" Mass, since it was my last day before leaving Maine for an extended time, when the inspiration struck me that I should sacrifice my preference and attend the other Mass. During a conversation with my friend after Mass, I was able to provide some helpful spiritual advice for a member of her family. Only God knows if, how, and why this advice may have been important to His designs.

Later that day, a regular summer visitor to the neighborhood whom I only casually knew came by with his very shy, dyslexic daughter, who had an interest in design. Observing the painters working on my house, she had given thought to what color my front door should be and offered a confident recommendation—red. I didn't have the heart to tell her that I had already purchased the door paint in another color, blue, but something told me that it would mean a whole lot to her if I followed her advice rather than sticking to my decision. So off I went to purchase red door paint.

These are embarrassingly miniscule examples, far from heroic acts of the spirit of obedience that many express in their daily lives. But they are clear examples of times when listening to the prompting of the Holy Spirit led me subjugate my will to another. In all honesty, I am often too distracted to pick up on the inspirations of the Holy Spirit, or, if I do, I swat them away, not wanting to detour from my own plans. In fact, this morning, before writing this section, the friend with whom I attended the Mass in Portland asked if I would join her and others, including a woman mourning the loss of her husband, for breakfast after Mass. I declined, as I felt impelled to work on this manuscript before the impending start of a new full-time job. I felt guilty for hours afterward and left my writing to go to confession.

The two great pitfalls for singles, including those who dedicate their lives to Christ, are selfishness and too great a love of independence. Most dedicated singles I know are quite independent by nature; they have to be in order to live on their own. One of the greatest challenges of the dedicated single vocation is reconciling a spirit of obedience with the independence required for a life lived alone in the world.

Poverty

Poverty is a richer concept than it appears at first blush. It begs to be understood in relative terms. Objective, or material, poverty in the developed world today means something entirely different from what it means in undeveloped areas, and also something entirely different from poverty as experienced two hundred, five hundred, or two thousand years ago. Mother Teresa, however, considered the developed world to be in the throes of the greatest poverty known to man—spiritual poverty—the despair of loneliness and feelings of being unloved.

Of the three evangelical counsels, poverty is one that lends itself most to misunderstanding. It is not a positive attribute in itself, and the poor are not necessarily better or holier than the rich. What the poor have over the rich is fewer obstacles hindering sanctity, less baggage to block them from entering through the narrow gate. Our fallen nature makes a proper attitude toward material goods difficult, and this fault can prove a major impediment to trusting in divine providence. "The danger of possessing riches is the carnal security to which they lead," said Blessed John Henry Newman, "that of desiring and pursuing them is that an object of this world is thus set before us as the aim and end of life."[112]

The evangelical counsel of poverty can be lived in a wide variety of ways. The history of the Church is replete with models, from the early desert hermits, such as St. Anthony of Egypt, to the fictitious, well-fed Friar Tuck, who personified certain monks and clerics who lived better than most common folks during the Middle

[112] John Henry Newman, *Parochial Sermons*, vol. 1 (New York: D. Appleton, 1843), 411.

Ages. An important impetus behind many of the reform movements throughout the Church's history was the desire to return to the gospel truth about the nature of material abundance: it tends to dampen religious fervor. One can love mammon or God, not both. Indeed, the history of the Franciscans is largely animated by various brothers branching off to return to their founder's example of lived poverty.

The medieval Dominicans had a more functional view of poverty, claiming that they did not preach because they were poor; they were poor because they preached. They did not own or have to administer large estates, so they could focus primarily on preaching and teaching.

It is good and fitting for religious to vow poverty as a way of following Christ's example. To live in the enclosed space of the monastery, renouncing everything, is a way of radically emptying themselves, as Jesus did to serve His Father wholeheartedly. Material poverty helps free the heart from created things and creatures. Modeling this detachment from material goods is especially important in today's culture of heightened consumerism.

But vowed material poverty is not fitting for most laity. In fact, the canon lawyers I know do not recommend that dedicated singles take even a "spiritual" vow of poverty. It is not concrete enough. The criteria by which one can judge whether one is living spiritual poverty is subjective, making it difficult to assess whether one is abiding by such a vow.

At the heart of the lay state is the call to leaven the world in its very midst. This necessitates owning and using temporal goods. Jesus did not expect radical poverty from all His early followers. His close friends Lazarus, Mary, and Martha were blessed with material wealth, which they dedicated to the service of the Kingdom.

It can be more difficult, however, to use material goods prudently than to renounce them altogether. Liberality is the little-known virtue of mastery over possessions. It is the golden mean between frugality and prodigality. "[Liberality] moderates the tendency to attachment among the wealthy, and tempers the natural fears which threaten the poor who must face present and future need with insufficient resources."[113] We must work to provide for the future and, at the same time, confidently abandon ourselves to God, knowing that He will provide.

> The soul of poverty is its spirit. This means a deep attachment to the providence of God, a trust in His eternal power and wisdom, a conviction that intimacy with Him [is] all the riches we intimately need. Poverty is really a cluster of virtues, beginning with the theological virtues, all actualized and reaching in my nothingness to Him as my All.[114]

Having spent well over twenty years traveling throughout Latin America, thanks to my work, I can say that some of the most generous, faith-filled, least materialistic people I've met are those with the fewest possessions, living in very challenging conditions. We should take care, however, not to glorify objective poverty. Living a life of material want or having to struggle to pay monthly bills can lead people to focus all their mental energies on temporal necessities. It can become a heavy burden, causing great strife and even compromised health.

What we should all strive for, religious and lay alike, is detachment from created things such that the things in our lives matter very little, if at all, beyond their ultimate purpose, which is to serve and glorify God. Paradoxically, those who are highly attached to possessions, fine dining, or luxurious vacations often take less

[113] Basil Cole, O.P., *A New Catechism of the Consecrated Life* (Bangalore, India: Asian Trading Corporation, 1997), 148.

[114] Ibid., 87.

delight in these things than those who regard them as unimportant. Or else, it takes an even more extravagant car, meal, or vacation to "satisfy" temporarily the insatiable desire of the heart.

Detachment frees the heart for God, disposing it for His favor. Detachment helps one to understand the truths of the Faith with greater clarity. The detached soul is able to apprehend the true value of things, seeing beyond their external appearances. Detachment paves the way for greater peace in the soul. This is not the detachment of Buddhists, who seek freedom from pain or a complete emptying of the mind. Detachment for a Christian means making room for God to rest in the heart.

Chapter 10

A Needed Witness Today

I am "the voice of one crying out in the desert, 'Make straight the way of the Lord.' "

—John 1:23

Let us beset the just one, because he is obnoxious to us; he sets himself against our doings. . . . To us he is the censure of our thoughts; merely to see him is a hardship for us, Because his life is not like that of others, and different are his ways.

—Wisd. 2:12–15

What the world is in particular need of today is the credible witness of people enlightened in mind and heart by the word of the Lord, and capable of opening the hearts and minds of many to the desire for God and for true life, life without end.

—Pope Benedict XVI, *Porta Fidei*, no. 15

I write this chapter on Gaudete (Rejoice) Sunday, which focuses on John the Baptist's great mission—proclaiming the imminent arrival of our Redeemer, Jesus Christ. John the Baptist prepared the hard, arid ground for Jesus. Even two thousand years ago, people were caught up in earthly affairs, indifferent to God, unaware that all was not well. The Baptist's role was to rattle the deadening complacency of those around him through prophetic words and through the example of his life. Without an introduction, Christ would have been too startling. The audience would not have been ready to hear His message.

Perhaps dedicated singles today may be able to play a similar role, helping those unable to respond to ordained priests or to religious, whose clerical clothing, habits, and radical way of life may be too bright for souls unused to the light.

Might the lights of dedicated singles, discretely twinkling throughout all walks of life, serve some special purpose in this historical moment that sorely lacks exemplary leadership?

Might dedicated singles—whose lives hearken back to the early Christian virgins, who attend daily Mass, and who fervently pray for priests—serve as a counterforce to clergy who have gone astray, empty churches, and doctrinal confusion?

Might dedicated singles—who do not fit into the traditional vocational categories but, rather, occupy a place that others view as undesirable—serve as an underground, revolutionary vanguard that builds up, rather than tears down?

Dedicated singles are leaven in the world. Through the integrity of their lives, they shine a light on what is true and beautiful, also revealing what is not. They are a dynamic, yet hidden force, evangelizing amid newly emerging, ever-changing secular spheres. They preach more loudly through their lives than through their words, empowered by what they accomplish in secret, through prayer and quiet sacrifice. By combining secular competence with a deeply Christian sensibility, dedicated singles are uniquely positioned to serve on the front lines of the Church's missionary outreach. Technology and globalization have placed a high premium on specialists, more so than during any time in history. Evangelization, therefore, calls for competent, well-formed, prayerful laypersons. Translating theological principles into the technological, financial, environmental, or medical spheres requires expertise, not presumption.

> It is not merely the "evil times" that prevent the clergy from penetrating as effectively into social structures as they did in earlier ages.... The layman who lives and works in these social milieus is not compensating for the clergy and religious but is in fact carrying out his proper apostolic function. The fact of his baptism and his confirmation authorizes him to carry out this function, which is rightly his own.[115]

In the early days of the Church, Christians brought something entirely new and revolutionary to pagan society. In today's post-modern culture, we are dealing with an ideological wasteland:

> We are confronted with those who cling to the deracinated shards of the Christian faith: Ideas that are genuinely Christian, like equality and justice and compassion, but ideas that have become disconnected to the concrete truth of Jesus Christ. And these rootless abstractions can turn deadly.... In some sense paganism would be easier to deal with than this set of deracinated convictions.[116]

In an age of abstractions, it may be the particularity and concreteness of individual, grace-filled lives that most effectively witnesses to Christ. In an age in which sexual depravity and arrogance reign, it may be humble and chaste people, rather than laws, that bring about greater humility and purity.

We live in a hypersexualized culture, and the prevalent sin of our day is one against purity. This sin is particularly offensive to God, since acts against purity affect our very bodies, which are temples of the Holy Trinity. What a sacrilege! Our Lady of Fatima

[115] Balthasar, *The Laity*, loc. 1413.

[116] Frederick C. Bauerschmidt, "Large and Startling Figures: Flannery O'Connor's Postmodern Apologetic," talk delivered at the Thomistic Institute, released on September 6, 2017.

warned about sins against purity, telling the three young seers of Fatima that more souls go to Hell due to sins of the flesh than for any other reason.

We should not underestimate the powerful witness of living out our Faith publicly. Something as seemingly basic as going to Mass on Sunday when we have visitors or are visiting someone can make a profound statement. I spent the night at a dear friend's house recently. She was raised Catholic and had been away from the Church for many years but had become increasingly open to returning. Without really thinking about it, I made plans to attend Sunday Mass the next morning and assumed she would come with me, as I always thought of her as a Catholic. She and her husband, who is not Catholic, did attend with me, and within two weeks she met with a priest, received the sacrament of confession, and is now actively practicing her Faith.

Something that has stuck with me is the comment I have heard made by a number of converts to the Catholic Faith. In response to the question "What took you so long?" they answered, "No one ever asked me to attend Mass with them."

Chapter 11

The Importance of Friendship for Dedicated Singles

Whoso feareth the Lord shall direct his friendship aright.

—Sirach 6:17, King James Version

If the bond of your mutual liking be charity, devotion, and Christian perfection, God knows how very precious a friendship is! Precious because it comes from God, because it tends to God, because God is the link that binds you, because it will last forever in Him.

Those who are living in the world require [holy friendships] for strength and comfort amid the difficulties which beset them. In the world all have not one aim, one mind, and therefore we must take to us congenial friends, nor is there any undue partiality in such attachments.

—St. Francis de Sales, *Introduction to the Devout Life*, pt. 3, chap. 19

Aquinas wrote that the essence of charity is friendship with God, and a side effect of this friendship with God is happiness. But how can we be a friend of God, since He is supernatural, and we are finite? Only through grace. The infinite distance has been bridged through grace, which raises us to the supernatural level.

Happiness is a consequence of an authentic, deeply held love of God, and this love flows out to others. We love concretely, through our emotions, bodies, temperaments, and decisions, not in a solely spiritually way, as angels do. We bring our sick friends hot chicken soup when they have a cold; we don't just wish them well from afar. God needs to have a primary place in our relationships with others. When this is not the case, our friendships need to be purified, just as our hope sometimes needs to be purified.

Authentic friendships have become rare in our culture. Too many "friendships" are merely relationships of utility or convenience, and they do not have mutual sanctity as their focus. All Christians serious about living out their baptismal vocations must carefully discern how and with whom to spend their precious time.

The solitary and unstructured nature of dedicated the single life makes Christian fellowship particularly important. Dedicated singles need mutual understanding and support from like-minded people who know the challenges and risks of this vocation. When we find ourselves among people who think like we do, we relax and feel that we belong, even though we may never have met before. It is as though we have known one another all our lives. The same goes for meeting others who live exclusively for Christ in the wider world. There tends to be an automatic understanding and appreciation. Fellow dedicated singles "get it" as few others do.

I previously mentioned how Justice Kennedy devalued celibacy with his assertion that, without same-sex marriage, people would be "condemned to live in loneliness." This mind-set also devalues deeply held, chaste friendships.

Chapter 12

Priests and Dedicated Singles

Priests are given the power to act *in persona Christi* (in the person of Christ) when they administer the sacraments. The spousal nature of the relationship between a dedicated single and Christ inspires a protective, prayerful attitude toward these priests, who are configured to Christ through ordination. Although consecrated religious, particularly cloistered ones, are among the most powerful prayer warriors for our priests, dedicated singles pray for priests and support them through apostolic work, hospitality, and other personal resources. Religious, consecrated laity, and dedicated singles typically have more time and mental space to pray for priests and for the Church.

St. Thérèse of Lisieux, like countless religious, saw prayer and sacrifice for priests as an integral part of her vocation. Though priests act *in persona Christi*, we know this doesn't mean they are perfect. St. Thérèse de Lisieux lived in a place, where priests were highly revered. During her eye-opening pilgrimage to Rome, however, she came to appreciate the vital importance of praying for priests' sanctity:

> Praying for sinners fascinated me, but praying for the souls of priests, whom I thought were purer than crystal, seemed strange to me! Ah! I understood my vocation in Italy [where]

> ... I lived with many holy priests for one month and understood that, if their sublime dignity lifts them above the angels, this does not mean that they are not weak and fragile.... This is the vocation of Carmel, because the only purpose of our prayers and our sacrifices is to be an apostle of the apostles, to pray for them whilst they evangelize souls by words and above all by example.[117]

St. Dominic placed great importance on the role of prayerful women in the support of his friars. Ten years before founding the Order of Preachers in 1216, St. Dominic established what would become the first convent of Dominican nuns expressly to pray for the sanctity and spiritual fecundity of his friars. Another powerful sign of the importance that Dominicans place on the complementary role of women in their order is a painting that hangs in the small chapel of Santa Maria Sopra Minerva in Rome. The three patronesses of the Dominican order—the Blessed Mother, St. Catherine of Alexandria, and Mary Magdalene—are represented in full glory holding up a portrait of St. Thomas Aquinas. I think the esteemed role of Mary Magdalene in this intellectual order is not solely because she was the great apostle of the apostles but also because of her passionate love for Jesus and His Blessed Mother. Preaching the Word of God with such love makes one's listeners more receptive to it.

The special calling to pray for and support the apostolic work of priests has its roots in Jesus' earthly ministry. The women surrounding Jesus and His apostles—Mary Magdalene, Joanna, Susanna, Mary, and Martha—played an essential role logistically, financially, and emotionally. They fed Jesus and the apostles with more than food; they supported their strenuous ministry with

[117] St. Thérèse de Lisieux, *Story of a Soul*, Manuscript A, 56r.

feminine gifts of maternal care, with prayer, with empathy, and with their joyful countenances. How Jesus and the apostles must have basked in and drawn strength from the loving sustenance of these female friends.

In another powerful example of supportive, God-centered friendships, St. Paul speaks fondly and appreciatively of his women collaborators—Apphia, Phoebe, Lydia of Philippi, Prisca, Aquila, Mary, Tryphaena, Tryphosa, Julia, Thecla, and Priscilla.

How critical it is today to pray for our priests! Instead of being revered, priests are often scorned, overworked, and subject to an aggressively sexualized culture. The priest abuse scandal and its many cover-ups are despicable. But in order not to lose faith, we have to remember two things. First, despicable behavior among its members has been part of the Church since its very foundation. In fact, Jesus allowed Judas to remain one of His chosen Twelve Apostles, knowing full well that Judas's heart had turned sour. Despite this, Jesus loved Judas to the very end.

Second, the Church comprises two complementary dimensions: the Petrine dimension, represented by the institutionalized hierarchy, and the Marian dimension, represented by the people. The health and fruitfulness of the Church depends on both dimensions prayerfully interceding for and supporting each other.

A historical example is instructive for our times. Once the Roman persecution ended in the fourth century, a great dilemma ensued. What was to be done with the apostates, those who had given up the sacred books and sacred vessels or betrayed brethren to the Romans, or who had renounced Christ directly? Ultimately, it was decided that they would undergo an extended penitential period.

It is little known, however, that the merits of those who had remained faithful during the persecution (those who were not martyred, of course) could be offered up to diminish the punishment of their fallen peers. It would be difficult to overestimate the hard feelings of those who held true to their Faith, losing so much in worldly terms, toward those who acted spinelessly, perhaps even treacherously, clinging to earthly goods or power. We must pray for and forgive our priests and bishops, and we must also demand accountability.

Particular Friendships with Priests

For millennia, authentic, deep friendships were held in high esteem, viewed as the noblest form of human communion and affection among laity and religious alike. True friendships, like marriages, help us grow in virtue and charity. So noble are human friendships, in fact, that they endure in heaven. For Aquinas, the three essential features of authentic friendships are benevolence (love of other), mutuality (reciprocity), and communication.

By the eighteenth century, "particular friendships" among religious had become largely frowned upon, due to legitimate concerns about cliquishness and the negative impact of errant friendships on community life.

Yet love must necessarily be preferential since we cannot love everyone equally. In fact, Aquinas described as "irrational" the idea that we love all others equally. Our ability to love deeply is limited to certain people. We have to be able to love some at a deeper level in order to love others well. It is natural and good that we love our own family members more deeply than social acquaintances, or our fellow citizens more than foreigners on another continent.

We are called to love all persons in view of God, but our responsibilities toward others and the ways our love manifests itself vary widely. Celibates, especially, are called to charitable love toward all, expecting little in the way of return. So it is through personal, reciprocal friendships, in which love and affection are exchanged, that all of us, including ordained and religious, receive emotional replenishment.[118]

Apart from praying for our priests, how advisable are friendships with priests, especially between priests and female celibates or between men and women in general, for that matter? Through His friendships with women, Jesus divinely sanctioned celibate friendship between men and women. But, clearly, human weakness did not threaten Jesus as it threatens us. Sadly, in today's sexualized epoch, a large and growing number of people are psychologically unable to form deep, healthy interpersonal relationships with the opposite sex. But for those who are emotionally mature, self-aware, and view God as their primary goal—friendships between male and female celibates is possible and deeply beneficial. If these critical conditions are not met, however, such a close friendship is imprudent and inadvisable.[119]

According to St. Francis de Sales, a true and "pure friendship is always the same—modest, courteous, and loving—knowing no change save an increasingly pure and perfect union, a type of the blessed friendships of Heaven."[120] For a priest who possesses this pure generous heart and who can exercise self-restraint for the good of the other in view God, a personal friendship can bring great benefit to himself and to countless others. The same goes for a vowed or consecrated religious or layperson:

> Mixed celibate friendship is desirable for two reasons. In the first place, it allows men and women, already sufficiently mature, to develop many other dimensions of

[118] Paul M. Conner, O.P., *Celibate Love* (Huntington, IN: Our Sunday Visitor, 1979), 29.

[119] See ibid., chaps. 1–2.

[120] Francis de Sales, *Introduction to the Devout Life* (New York: Random House, 2002), 134.

> their human potential, some of which normally blossom only through relationships with persons of the opposite sex. Through each other, their own individualities are authentically actualized, and by the complementing richness of the other, each friend attains psychic and spiritual "fullness of humanity." As a consequence, these enriched persons are more capable of loving God and all men with genuine human love.[121]

Paul M. Conner, O.P., makes the case, in his book *Celibate Love*, that the highly developed masculine aspects of Western civilization, such as science, technology, and industry have made for an overly masculine ethos. The result is a "malaise [that] is currently reflected in the alarming number of people who suffer from the inability adequately to know and love one another or God."[122] A friendship between mature and self-aware vowed persons of the opposite sex can help each more fully develop loving relations with God. The man learns self-sacrifice and how to be more receptive to God's love, and the woman gains deeper insight into divine love's more masculine qualities, such as protectiveness, strength, and justice.

Profound friendships in view of God—such as those of St. Francis de Sales and St. Jane Frances de Chantal, or Bl. Jordan of Saxony and Bl. Diana d'Andalo, or St. Catherine of Siena and Bl. Raymond of Capua, or St. Teresa of Avila and Fr. Jerome Gracian—are richly edifying, spiritually and temporally fruitful, and rare. The eschewing of private interactions between the sexes for prudential reasons is understandable in today's sexualized, "me too" environment. Much is lost, though.

[121] Conner, *Celibate Love*, 46.
[122] Ibid., 127.

The Need for Priests to Encourage Prayer in Parishes

> We must also remember the great number of *single persons* who, because of the particular circumstances in which they have to live—often not of their choosing—are especially close to Jesus' heart and therefore deserve the special affection and active solicitude of the Church, especially of pastors. Many remain *without a human family* often due to conditions of poverty. Some live their situation in the spirit of the Beatitudes, serving God and neighbor in exemplary fashion. The doors of homes, the "domestic churches," and of the great family which is the Church must be open to all of them. "No one is without a family in this world: the Church is a home and family for everyone, especially those who 'labor and are heavy laden.'"[123]

Many experience raw emotional pains for not having married. These souls would be well served by spiritual guidance, by priests, religious or well-formed laity, to help them embrace their baptismal vocation and to discern whether Jesus might be calling them to a permanent spousal union with Him in the world.

This may be less obvious, but another way that priests could support dedicated singles is by visibly modelling personal prayer for their parishioners. What a powerful and welcome message it would send to married and single laity, alike, to see our priests praying before the tabernacle or leading a Rosary before or after Mass. When I suggested this to a young priest, he expressed hesitation in joining the "old-lady" Rosary brigade, sensitive to interjecting himself in a lay-driven prayer custom. On the contrary! How we

[123] *Catechism of the Catholic Church*, no. 1658; *Familiaris Consortio* 85; cf. Matt. 11:28.

would welcome priestly participation in this powerful devotion, and how it would encourage more to spend an extra few minutes on their knees after having just received Christ — the most important and spiritually powerful moment of our day. A great frustration for me and for contemplative laity I know is the noise and lack of prayerful recollection in Churches.

Priests should encourage reverent, prayerful silence in Church before and after Mass. Silence is a rare commodity these days, even in churches! A roar of whispers and *sotto voce* conversations drown out the peace before and after Mass, even daily Mass. As someone sensitive to noise, despite my feeble hearing, this is agitating. During one such post-daily-Mass conversation I overheard, which grew from *sotto voce* to *forte*, it became apparent to me that Christ in the tabernacle yearns deeply for our full attention. Yet many of us engage in nonprayerful conversations, neglectful of Jesus, who is physically in our midst, waiting patiently for our attention and our love.

I also wonder whether chattering in church is any different from allowing one's thoughts to scamper about, disengaged from God, despite His being right there with us in the tabernacle? Stewing in the mundane, in fantasy, or in planning during designated prayer times, or in the direct presence of God in the tabernacle, is very Martha-like. Being Martha on all too many occasions myself has made me a bit more patient with church chatterers — but not much.

Chapter 13

Why "A Hidden Joy"?

I give praise to your holy nature, Lord, for you have made my nature a sanctuary for your hiddenness and a tabernacle for your Mysteries.[124]

Where does [joy] come from? How is it to be explained? Certainly, there are many factors at work here. But in my view, the crucial one is this certainty, based on faith: I am wanted; I have a task in history; I am accepted, I am loved. . . . Faith makes one happy from deep within."

—Benedict XVI, Christmas Greeting to the Roman Curia, December 22, 2011

The subtitle of this book, *A Hidden Joy in the Catholic Church*, came to me when I began discerning a pull to embark on this writing project. So much of the spiritual life is hidden. God is the ultimate hidden mystery, whom we experience through faith. The potential for experiencing great joy while living out one's baptismal vocation as a dedicated single is also widely unknown—hidden, if you will.

[124] Isaac of Nineveh, *Homélies Ascétiques*, trans. Sebastian Brock (Louvain: Peeters Publishers, 1995), 8.

Hidden

> Brothers and sisters: If then you were raised with Christ, seek what is above, where Christ is seated at the right hand of God. Think of what is above, not of what is on earth. For you have died, and your life is hidden with Christ in God. When Christ your life appears, then you too will appear with Him in glory. (Col. 3:1–4)

One of the great paradoxes of our Christian Faith is that God is both all powerful and hidden at the same time. Most of the time, God operates in a hidden way—hidden to many, but not to all.

There were moments during Christ's time on earth when God majestically revealed Himself; for example, at Christ's baptism and at the Transfiguration. And during the first thirty years of His life, working in obscurity in a workshop in Nazareth, the Son of God was also hidden—so hidden that His fellow townsmen were scandalized when Jesus began preaching and performing miracles: "Where did this man get all this?" (Matt. 13:56).

The dedicated-single vocation is a hidden one. Many, if not most, dedicated singles do not advertise their spousal relationship with Christ. But hidden away in countless workplaces around the world, dedicated singles serve as sanctifying leaven, as small glimmering lights. Mother Teresa never tired of saying, "Performing small acts with great love is all God asks of us."

Hidden things come to be valued gradually. That flashy person or object that immediately captures our attention also quickly bores us. But that person or thing that we only gradually come to notice, because on the surface there is nothing to grab our attention, often reveals beautiful, multifaceted elements that keep us intrigued.

Only eleven people attended St. Thérèse of Lisieux's funeral. The richness of her life was so hidden that the mother superior of her convent wasn't sure she could adequately fill an obituary notice with enough events from her life. St. Thérèse was canonized only twenty-eight years after her death and was declared a Doctor of the Church one hundred years after her death. Today she is one of our most beloved saints.

Cloistered nuns and monks are hidden spiritual intercessors and warriors. They are separated from the world, but their convents are visible signs of God's presence in the world. Habited religious with active apostolates are visible signs of God's work in the world. Dedicated singles, in contrast, are completely hidden, yet in plain sight, in the world.

So much of God's work is hidden. Few are aware of Jesus' hidden sixth wound on His shoulder. Jesus told St. Faustina that the worst physical pain He endured during His Passion was the unspeakable pain of carrying the cross on His shoulder, which had been ripped apart during His brutal scourging. Asked which of his stigmata was the most painful, Padre Pio is known to have answered that it was the one on his shoulder. And to think that Simon of Cyrene initially refused to accompany Jesus and help support the very Cross causing Him such pain! How much pain do we cause Jesus when we reject our own crosses? How many of us is Jesus calling to accompany Him shoulder to shoulder amid the commotion of the world?

God's hiddenness screamed to me when I entered a certain church in Maine for the first time after having driven by it dozens of times. From the outside, an uglier church could not have been conceived. More than ugly, it is downright scary. Flanking a sort of tower, facing the street, is a huge mural of a Star-Wars-looking character—not handsome Hans Solo or Luke Skywalker, but one of the creepy characters. Taking a wild guess, I assumed this was an "artist's" rendering of Jesus. Inside the church, however, is another story. The interior is of modern design, but reverent nonetheless. The focal point is an unusual, large crucifix with the body of the crucified Jesus not slumped but, rather, powerfully projected forward.

Here is Jesus who is not resigned to His horrific fate, but one who assertively embraces it.

Joy

When asked what God does all day, our greatest Catholic theologian, St. Thomas Aquinas, answered, "He enjoys Himself!" God's sheer joy in Himself, in the Trinity, begs to be shared with us, and we can partake of this joy if we choose. "I have told you these things that my joy may be in you and your joy may be complete" (John 15:11). Indeed, the first word of the first psalm is "happy." God wants us to be happy—joyful—and He provides us with the road map to reach this destination.

"Joy ... is nothing else than a delight of the will in an object esteemed and considered fitting."[125] We experience true, lasting joy only when we make God our supreme good, not just intellectually, but deep in our hearts. We all have something that reigns supreme, something around which everything else revolves. Even if it is something objectively good—such as marriage, children, an edifying career, financial security, health, esteem of others—it will block us from achieving true joy because none of these things are our ultimate purpose. Unless God reigns supreme in our minds and hearts, joy and its complement, peace, will elude us.

The writings of St. John of the Cross are a powerful antidote to the anodyne spirituality reigning in the cushioned-pew, low-ceiling churches of today. The "Doctor of Nada" provides us with a detailed, unvarnished roadmap of the ascent toward union with God, the path *all* of us are called to tread during our earthly sojourn. The greatest danger along this path, St. John warns, is becoming distracted by, or too focused on, the relatively hollow joys of temporal goods. The most profound and lasting joy possible is to be

[125] *The Collected Works of St. John of the Cross*, 294.

found in God. Undue attachment to virtually anything or anyone else gives rise to anxiety.

I was baptized in a tiny church, in a tiny town, Kingstree, South Carolina. From my mother's telling, I screamed throughout the baptism, inspiring the priest to make a quip about the meek inheriting the earth. Many years later, this church was dedicated as a diocesan shrine called Our Lady of Joyful Hope.

At a certain point, having read about the importance of celebrating one's baptismal anniversary, I was inspired to return to the site where I became a daughter of God. My parents and I made a little pilgrimage to Our Lady of Joyful Hope, and it was this visit that helped me appreciate how important joy is to our Christian vocation. I had been driven and hardworking for so many years up to this point, and joy just didn't seem that important. In fact, it had seemed a bit frivolous.

At about that time, I was reading St. Thérèse of Lisieux's *Story of a Soul*, which beautifully extolls the importance of joy in our relationship with God. St. Thérèse was declared a Doctor of the Church partly for her simple but profound insight into an essential quality of God's love for us—joy. God takes great joy in His children, and He wants us to share in this joy. St. Thérèse spent her short life offering God moments of joy, even fun, sometimes imagining herself as a toy for the Infant Jesus.

At first, St. Thérèse's imaginings of herself as an object of joy for the Baby Jesus struck me as cute and heartwarming. Only later have I come to appreciate how profound and, indeed, revolutionary St. Thérèse's spirituality is, especially coming from a region and epoch mired in Jansenism.

Fr. Wojciech Giertych, O.P., who has a special appreciation for St. Thérèse and, of course, for St. Thomas Aquinas—a seeming paradox but, in fact, a profound synthesis of our Faith—spoke powerfully of Christian joy at a 2016 women's retreat. He explained that God is joy, a dynamic joy that gives and receives between the three Persons of the Trinity. Divine love wants to give, wants to expand. Creating the world and its creatures was a great moment of joy for God. God enjoys His creation and wants us to share in this joy, as His children. St. Thérèse knew this intuitively, teaching us to open ourselves to God's love not out of obedience, but for God's very pleasure. St. Thérèse gave joy to God, moment by moment. Our work in the spiritual life is to do the same through our cooperation with God.

It is a lot easier to be receptive to God's love and to trust in Him if we view ourselves as small children looking up to a joyful, doting father, rather than a stern taskmaster always ready to punish. For St. Thérèse, being small in front of God meant never being discouraged. After all, small children frequently fall but their parents are there to console them. We are His beloved children despite our flaws and mistakes. We cannot earn God's love. God relishes our littleness because it makes us more receptive to His love. Our work in the spiritual life is to cooperate and increase our receptivity to God, giving Him joy. In turn, this gives *us* great joy. Sanctity does not consist in behaving perfectly or in being in a perpetual emotionally mellow state but, rather, in placing our weakness in the powerful, loving hands of God.

Chapter 14

Final Thought

History unfolds, not in a Hegelian deterministic way, but through the unpredictable, countless acts of countless individuals responding to grace (or not). There is an incarnational quality to this working of grace in the historical narrative. Today grace is being incarnated through the lives of dedicated singles clinging to Christ, keeping Him company, providing Him joy in little corners of the world.

Could there be new expressions of faith that are taking shape at this moment in salvation history? Could dedicated singles be the note that God has composed for these troubled times that scream out for sanctity and even heroism?

> New times [demand] new answers and new solutions, solutions that do not supplant earlier ones, but rather aid them, interpret them, and inspire them, as the last note of a melody to be played explains the previous notes and makes clear the unity of the whole melody. But it is only at the end of time that the entire melody, as it was composed by the Holy Spirit and unfolded through the centuries, will be complete and thus fully comprehensible. It is the task of the present day to grasp as purely as possible the note that must be played

> today, the divine word that must be spoken today, and to incarnate it as obediently as possible.[126]

What I have tried to convey here is how God's love may be unfolding in individual lives today. Perhaps over time greater ecclesial or juridical recognition of the dedicated-single vocation will develop, offering a guiding structure. After all, the reality of the spiritual life precedes canon law. The twentieth century witnessed the flowering of consecrated lay vocations expressed through newly sanctioned secular institutes. Perhaps we are waiting for the Church to catch up to grace, whereby the twenty-first century may witness the flowering of a more widely understood and sanctioned dedicated single vocation.

[126] Balthasar, *The Laity*, loc. 1301.

Appendix I

Discerning a Vocation to Consecrated Virginity versus Dedicated Single

The following is from the *Sponsa Christi* blog,[127] written by Jenna Marie Cooper, a consecrated virgin with advanced degrees in theology and canon law:

> Generally speaking a woman may have a vocation to consecrated virginity if she:
>
> - feels a definite, specific call to live and be known as a spouse of Christ with an explicitly "bridal" spirituality
> - feels called to a life of public witness and is willing and able to be open about her vocation at all times and with everyone she meets
> - feels a special attraction to the Liturgy of the Hours and is willing and able to recite the Divine Office every day
> - feels called to live a demonstrably "consecrated" lifestyle and is willing and able to live in the spirit of evangelical poverty and obedience

[127] "Consecrated Virginity versus Private Vows," *Sponsa Christi* (blog), December 16, 2010, http://sponsa-christi.blogspot.it/2010/12/consecrated-virginity-versus-private.html.

- feels called to devote her life to work which directly advances the Church's mission
- feels a special spiritual bond with the local church and is willing and able to spend her life at the service of God's people within the diocese where she is to be consecrated
- is emotionally well-balanced, in good mental health, and has adequate social skills (i.e., she could have lived community)
- is willing and able to learn and to be open to formation

On the other hand, my thought is that simply making a lifelong, private vow of virginity would be a better course of action for a woman who

- feels called to live as a spouse of Christ but in a subtle, more "under the radar"-type way
- OR feels that her own individual call to be a bride of Christ is essentially a personal matter between herself and the Lord, and thus something which should involve only a very minimal degree of formal structure or official recognition
- OR feels a special call to "evangelize the world from within" as a "hidden leaven" in the midst of secular society
- OR feels called to offer her heart entirely to Christ, while at the same time using her gifts to strive for excellence within a purely secular career
- OR feels that her primary vocation (i.e., that around which she is to order her life and base all her major decisions) is to some particular apostolic work, and therefore sees a spousal relationship with Christ as a somewhat "secondary" vocation but still desires to offer herself to Christ in a way that excludes human marriage
- OR feels that her primary vocation, or at least a significant component of her call to be a bride of Christ, is

membership to the secular third order of a religious community (quick fact: St. Catherine of Siena actually was NOT a consecrated virgin but was instead a lay third-order Dominican who made a private vow of perpetual virginity).

Because private vows are, in essence, a wholly personal and individual response to the love of God, there are as many ways to live out a private vow of virginity as there are souls who are called to profess one.

Appendix II

Sample Vows for the Dedicated Single

Canon law defines private vows but does not regulate them or offer any stipulations or guidelines concerning them. Private vows are a very personal thing between God and the soul. Canon lawyers with whom I've spoken strongly encourage vowing only objective, concrete commitments, such that it is very clear whether they are being met. Here is a sample of a private vow:

> Most Sacred Heart of Jesus, I now dedicate my whole person, body and soul, to You as my Divine Spouse, to live in perfect chastity for ______ year(s) (or: my whole life), that I may please You more perfectly by a holy life, that I may enjoy more intimate and intense happiness with You in the glorious life of heaven, and that I may be able to help a greater number of fellow men to procure for themselves a peaceful life on earth and everlasting happiness in heaven. Amen.[128]

Before taking her private vow in June 2016, this friend wrote to me:

> I find this all very exciting at this special point and time in my life's journey. The timing of this and the particular

[128] Dominic J. Unger, O.F.M. Cap., *The Mystery of Love for the Single* (Rockford, IL: TAN Books, 2005).

step seem so right and good! I feel so ready for this now! So happy and excited! More and more in love with Our Lord! Like a young bride about to be married to her cherished Beloved! I am also realizing that "preparation" for this has been happening for many years. This is not something totally new—it is the blossoming of something that has been growing, developing, and slowly maturing for a long time. And I have loved Our Lord all my life. It is not as if I just met Him for the first time recently and now want to join my life with His. I have known Him for a very long time. He is my closest Companion, as is His Mother. What's more, I have always had a sense that *I belong to Him*, that *I am His*. Perhaps I did not express it or live it so well, but I long to live it beautifully now.

I am sensing that there are divine graces being poured forth even in preparation for these vows! It is as if Our Lord and Our Blessed Mother are smiling already—even before it actually takes place, even in simply pondering and preparing for it! And the thought of making THEM smile makes me smile! I want to please Them both very much—not just a little bit, but mightily! With the help of Their grace, of course!

Here is a portion of her vows, written herself, taken in June 2016:

I, (Name), take You, my Lord and Savior Jesus Christ, to be my Chosen and Beloved Spouse—to have and to hold from this day forward. I promise to be faithful and true to Your Divine Majesty in good times and in bad, for richer or for poorer, in sickness and in health, and, by Your most merciful and gracious gift of Yourself, even death shall never part us, but shall unite us even more closely for all eternity.

I shall love You and honor You, worship You and adore You, respect You and listen to You, cherish and obey Your Holy Word, serve You and stay united with You as beautifully and closely as I possibly can all the days of my life, and throughout everlasting life.

I entrust my whole life and heart to You through the Immaculate Heart of Mary, Your Most Holy Mother.

[The priest, *in persona Christi*]: (Name), take this ring as a sign of Our Lord's love and fidelity in the name of the Father, and of the Son, and of the Holy Spirit. Amen.

"My spirit finds JOY in God my Savior!"

Finally, here is my vow, which I composed:

Jesus, I give myself to You. My entire heart I offer to You, to no one else and to no work which would divide my heart. I want only You. Do with me as You will. Help me to depend on Your grace—not on my own feeble efforts—to keep me close to Your Sacred, loving, burning Heart.

Father, carry me at Your breast this year. Keep me close. Do not let my heart get filled with busyness and activity, as is my wont.

Holy Spirit, animate my soul. Fill me with Your wisdom. Help me discern the best way to please and love Jesus.

Blessed Mother, I consecrate myself to your Immaculate Heart. Help me to love your Son as He deserves to be loved. Please ask Jesus to shower down on me the necessary graces to make me His worthy spouse. Walk with me, Mary. Protect me from the snares of the devil. Stomp on his deceitful head so that he has no power over me!

I wear this ring, Jesus, to be always reminded of Your love for me and as a sign of my love for You.

SINGLE FOR A GREATER PURPOSE

The Spiritual Canticle

En la interior bodega
de mi Amado, bebí, y cuando
salía
por toda aquesta vega,
ya cosa no sabía;
y el ganado perdí que antes
seguía.

In the inner wine cellar
I drank of my Beloved, and,
when I went abroad
through all this valley,
I no longer knew anything,
and lost the herd that I was
following.

Allí me dio su pecho,
allí me enseñó ciencia muy
sabrosa;
y yo le di de hecho
a mí, sin dejar cosa;
allí le prometi de ser su Esposa.

There he gave me his breast;
there he taught me a sweet and
living knowledge;
and I gave myself to him,
keeping nothing back;
there I promised to be his bride.

Mi alma se ha empleado,
y todo mi caudal en su servicio;

ya no guardo ganado,
ni ya tengo otro oficio,
que ya sólo en amar es mi
ejercicio.

Now I occupy my soul
and all my energy in his service;
I no longer tend the herd,
nor have I any other work
now that my every act is love.

Pues ya si en el ejido
de hoy más no fuere vista ni
hallada,
diréis que me he perdido;
que, andando enamorada,
me hice perdidiza, y fui ganada.

If, then, I am no longer
seen or found on the common,
you will say that I am lost;
that, stricken by love,
I lost myself, and was found.[129]

[129] Verses 17–20 of the first redaction or 26–29 of the second redaction, in *The Collected Works of St. John of the Cross*, 47, 78.

Appendix III

Bible Passages concerning Singles

Holy Scripture, especially the epistles of St. Paul, extols the spiritual advantages of celibacy. Here are a few particularly relevant passages.

> Some are incapable of marriage because they were born so; some, because they were made so by others; some, because they have renounced marriage for the sake of the kingdom of heaven. Whoever can accept this ought to accept it. (Matt. 19:12)

> Jesus said to them, "The children of this age marry and remarry; but those who are deemed worthy to attain to the coming age and to the resurrection of the dead neither marry nor are given in marriage. They can no longer die, for they are like angels; and they are the children of God because they are the ones who will rise. (Luke 20:34–36)

> Now concerning the unmarried, I have no command of the Lord, but I give my opinion as one who by the Lord's mercy is trustworthy. I think that in view of the impending distress it is well for a person to remain as he is. (1 Cor. 7:25–27, RSVCE)

> I want you to be free from anxieties. The unmarried man is anxious about the affairs of the Lord, how to please the

Lord; but the married man is anxious about worldly affairs, how to please his wife, and his interests are divided. And the unmarried woman or girl is anxious about the affairs of the Lord, how to be holy in body and spirit; but the married woman is anxious about worldly affairs, how to please her husband." (1 Cor. 7:32–34, RSVCE)

A wife is bound to her husband as long as he lives. If the husband dies, she is free to be married to whom she wishes, only in the Lord. But in my judgment, she is happier if she remains as she is. And I think that I have the Spirit of God." (1 Cor. 7:39–40, RSVCE)

"Now to the unmarried and to widows, I say: it is a good thing for them to remain as they are, as I do." (1 Cor. 7:8)

Appendix IV

Reflections of Venerable Madeleine Delbrêl

There are some people whom God takes and sets apart.

There are others He leaves among the crowds, people He does not "withdraw from the world."

These are the people who have an ordinary job, an ordinary household, or an ordinary celibacy. People with ordinary sicknesses and ordinary times of grieving. People with an ordinary house and ordinary clothes. These are the people of ordinary life. The people we might meet on any street.

They love the door that opens onto the street, just as their brothers who are hidden from the world love the door that shuts behind them forever.

We, the ordinary people of the streets, believe with all our might that this street, this world, where God has placed us, is our place of holiness.

We believe that we lack nothing here that we need. If we needed something else, God would already have given it to us.

We do not need to find silence; we already have it. The day we lack silence is the day we have not learned how to keep it.

All the noises around us cause much less disturbance than we ourselves do.

The real noise is the echo things make within us. . . .

Monasteries appear to be the place of praise and the place of the silence that praise requires.

In the street, crushed by the crowd, we make our souls into so many caves of silence wherein the Word of God can dwell and resound.

In those crowds marked by the sins of hatred, lust, and drunkenness, we find a desert of silence, and we recollect ourselves here with great ease, so that God can ring out His name: *Vox clamantis in deserto*.[130]

[130] Madeleine Delbrêl, *We, the Ordinary People of the Streets*, trans. David Louis Schindler Jr. and Charles F. Mann (Grand Rapids: Wm. B. Eerdmans, 2000), 54–58.

Selected Bibliography

Apostoli, Andrew, C.F.R. *When God Asks for an Undivided Heart: Choosing Celibacy in Love and Freedom*. Irving, TX: Basilica Press, 2007.

Aumann, Jordan, O.P. *Christian Spirituality in the Catholic Tradition*. San Francisco: Ignatius Press, 1985.

———. *On the Front Lines: The Lay Person in the Church after Vatican II*. Staten Island, NY: Alba House, 1990.

Autor, David, David Dorn, and Gordon Hansen. "When Work Disappears: Manufacturing Decline and the Failing Marriage-Market Value of Men." NBER Working Paper 23173, February 2017.

Balthasar, Hans Urs von. *The Christian State of Life*. Translated by Sr. Mary Frances McCarthy. San Francisco: Ignatius Press, 1983.

———. *The Laity and the Life of the Counsels: The Church's Mission in the World*. San Francisco: Ignatius Press, 2003. Kindle Cloud.

Benedictine Monk. *In Sinu Jesu: When Heart Speaks to Heart*. Kettering, OH: Angelico Press, 2016.

Berthier, Rev. Jean-Baptiste. *States of the Christian Life and Vocation: According to the Doctors and Theologians of the Church*. New York: P. O'Shea, 1879.

Bolin, Joseph, *Paths of Love: The Discernment of Vocation according to the Teaching of Aquinas, Ignatius, and Pope John Paul II*. Self-published, CreateSpace, 2008.

Boudway, Matthew, and Grant Gallicho. "An Interview with Cardinal Walter Kasper." *Commonweal*, May 7, 2014.

Caldecott, Leonie. "In Good Hands: Caryll Houselander and the Single Vocation." *Humanum: Issues in Family, Culture, and Science* 2 (2017).

Cantalamessa, Raniero, O.F.M. Cap. *Virginity: A Positive Approach to Celibacy for the Sake of the Kingdom of Heaven*. Staten Island, NY: Society of St. Paul, 1995.

Chautard, Jean-Baptiste, O.C.S.O. *The Soul of the Apostolate*. Charlotte, NC: TAN Books, 2012.

Ciszek, Walter J., S.J. *He Leadeth* Me. San Francisco: Ignatius Press, 1995.

Cole, Basil, O.P. A *New Catechism of the Consecrated Life: Help for Perplexed Postulants and Novices of the Third Millennium*. Bangalore, India: Asian Trading Corporation, 1997.

Cole, Basil, O.P., and Conner, Paul, O.P., *Christian Totality: Theology of the Consecrated Life*, New York: Alba House, 1997.

Conner, Paul M., O.P., *Celibate Love*. Huntington, IN: Our Sunday Visitor, 1979.

Delbrêl, Venerable Madeleine. *We, the Ordinary People of the Streets*. Translated by David Louis Schindler Jr. and Charles F. Mann. Grand Rapids: Wm. B. Eerdmans, 2000.

de l'Enfant Jesus, P. Marie-Eugène, O.C.D. *I Am a Daughter of the Church*. Vol. 2, Notre Dame, IN: Christian Classics, 1995.

———. *Where the Spirit Breathes*. Translated by Sr. Mary Thomas Noble, O.P., Philippines: Society of St. Paul, 2007.

de Sales, Francis. *Introduction to the Devout Life*. New York: Random House, 2002.

de Yepes y Álvarez, St. John (of the Cross). *The Collected Works of St. John of the Cross*. Translated by Kieran Kavanaugh, O.C.D., and Otilio Rodriguez, O.C.D. Washington, D.C.: Institute of Carmelite Studies, 1991.

Dubay, Thomas, S.M. *". . . And You Are Christ's": The Charism of Virginity and the Celibate Life*. San Francisco: Ignatius Press, 1987.

———. *Seeking Spiritual Direction: How to Grow the Divine Life Within*. Cincinnati: Servant Books, 1993.

Echivard, Nicole. *Femme, Qui Es-Tu?* Paris: Criterion, 1985.

Escrivá de Balaguer, St. Josemaría. *Conversations with Monsignor Josemaría Escrivá*. Princeton: Scepter Publishers, 2002.

Francis, Pope. Post-Synodal Apostolic Exhortion *Amoris Laetitia* (March 19, 2016)

Giertych, Wojciech, O.P. "Prayer and Celibacy: The Apostolic Origin of Priestly Celibacy." *The Priest* (September 2011): 79–88.

———. "The Virtue of Chastity in Marriage: Its Reality and Difficulties." *Doctor Communis* Annuario/2 della Pontificia Accademia di San Tommaso d'Aquino: *San Tommaso il matrimonio e la famiglia* a cura di Serge-Thomas Bonino e Guido Mazzota (Città del Vaticano: Urbaniania University Press, 2019).

Haggerty, Fr. Donald. *Conversion: Spiritual Insights into an Essential Encounter with God*. San Francisco: Ignatius Press, 2017.

Heaney, Stephen J. "On Good and Evil in the Things That Afflict Us." *Homiletic and Pastoral Review*, November 6, 2017.

Houselander, Caryll. *The Reed of God*. Notre Dame, IN: Ave Maria Press, 2006.

John Paul II, Pope. Post-Synodal Apostolic Exhortation *Christifideles Laici* (December 30, 1988).

———. Post-Synodal Apostolic Exhortation *Vita Consecrata* (March 25, 1996).

———. *Words of Inspiration: The Private Prayers of Pope John Paul II*. New York: Simon and Schuster, 2001.

Keane, Judy. *Single and Catholic: Finding Meaning in Your State of Life*. Manchester, NH: Sophia Institute Press, 2016.

Marmion, Blessed Columba. *Christ: The Life of the Soul*. Bethesda, MD: Zaccheus Press, 2005.

Martin, St. Thérèse (of Lisieux). *Story of a Soul*. Translated by John Clarke. Washington, D.C.: Institute of Carmelite Studies, 1976.

McKinsey and Company. "Jobs Lost, Jobs Gained: Workforce Transitions in a Time of Automation." December 2017.

Peters, Edward N., J.D., J.C.D., "My Q&A on 'Continence,' 'Celibacy,' and 'Chastity.' *In the Light of the Law* (blog), January 15, 2015.

Philippe, Jacques. *Fire and Light: Learning to Receive the Gift of God*. New York: Scepter Publishers, 2016.

———. *Interior Freedom*. New York: Scepter Publishers, 2007.

Pius XII, "Address to Italian Women." (October 21, 1945).

———. Motu Proprio *Primo Feliciter* (March 12, 1948).

———. Apostolic Constitution *Provida Mater Ecclesia* (February 2, 1947).

———. Encyclical *Sacra Virginitas* (March 25,1954).

Reeves, Richard V., and Dimitrios Halikias. "Are Chinese Factories Really Killing Marriage in America?" Brookings Institute, March 10, 2017.

Regneris, Mark. *Cheap Sex: The Transformation of Men, Marriage, and Monogamy*. New York: Oxford University Press, 2017.

Rodríguez, Pedro, Fernando Ocáriz, and José Luis Illanes. *Opus Dei in the Church*. Dublin: Four Courts Press, 1994.

Sandberg, Sheryl. *Lean In: Women, Work, and the Will to Lead*. New York: Alfred A. Knopf, 2017.

Second Vatican Council. Pastoral Constitution on the Church in the Modern World *Gaudium et Spes* (December 7, 1965).

Snow, Patricia. "Dismantling the Cross." *First Things* (April 2015).

Stein, Edith. *Essays on Woman*. Washington, D.C.: ICS Publications, 1996.

Sullivan, Patricia A., "The Nonvowed Form of the Lay State in the Life of the Church." *Theological Studies* 68, no. 2 (June 2007): 320–347.

Swanson, Ana. "144 Years of Marriage and Divorce in the United States, in One Chart." *Washington Post*, June 23, 2015.

Traister, Rebecca. "Single Women Are Now the Most Potent Political Force." *New York Magazine*, February 22, 2016.

Unger, Dominic J., O.F.M. Cap. *The Mystery of Love for the Single: A Guide for Those Who Follow the Single Vocation in the World.* Rockford, IL: TAN Books, 2005.

Vanier, Jean. *Becoming Human*. New York: Paulist Press, 1998.

von Hildebrand, Dietrich. *In Defense of Purity*. Steubenville, OH: Hildebrand Project, 2017.

About the Author

Luanne D. Zurlo is executive director of the Brilla public charter school network and voluntary afterschool Catholic faith formation program in the South Bronx. Prior to joining Seton Education Partners in January 2018, Luanne taught finance, Catholic social doctrine, and educational reform in developing countries at the Catholic University of America. She spent much of her early career working with Latin America as a ranked Wall Street equity analyst. After experiencing 9/11 firsthand, she left Goldman Sachs and founded a not-for-profit organization, Educando, whose mission is to raise educational quality in Latin America, with a special focus on Brazil and Mexico. Luanne has lived, studied, and worked extensively in Latin America and Europe. She has an MBA in finance and accounting from Columbia Business School, an MA in international affairs from Johns Hopkins University SAIS, and a BA in history from Dartmouth College. Luanne serves on a number of boards for Catholic organizations and lives in New York City, spending as much time as she can in Falmouth, Maine.

Sophia Institute

Sophia Institute is a nonprofit institution that seeks to nurture the spiritual, moral, and cultural life of souls and to spread the Gospel of Christ in conformity with the authentic teachings of the Roman Catholic Church.

Sophia Institute Press fulfills this mission by offering translations, reprints, and new publications that afford readers a rich source of the enduring wisdom of mankind.

Sophia Institute also operates the popular online resource CatholicExchange.com. *Catholic Exchange* provides world news from a Catholic perspective as well as daily devotionals and articles that will help readers to grow in holiness and live a life consistent with the teachings of the Church.

In 2013, Sophia Institute launched Sophia Institute for Teachers to renew and rebuild Catholic culture through service to Catholic education. With the goal of nurturing the spiritual, moral, and cultural life of souls, and an abiding respect for the role and work of teachers, we strive to provide materials and programs that are at once enlightening to the mind and ennobling to the heart; faithful and complete, as well as useful and practical.

Sophia Institute gratefully recognizes the Solidarity Association for preserving and encouraging the growth of our apostolate over the course of many years. Without their generous and timely support, this book would not be in your hands.

www.SophiaInstitute.com
www.CatholicExchange.com
www.SophiaInstituteforTeachers.org

Sophia Institute Press® is a registered trademark of Sophia Institute.
Sophia Institute is a tax-exempt institution as defined by the Internal Revenue Code, Section 501(c)(3). Tax ID 22-2548708.

SPIRITUAL GROWTH $18.95

Joyfully single ... nourishing the world and the Church

In these fascinating pages, author Luanne Zurlo shows that, contrary to popular opinion, single life is often a holy, joyful vocation lived out, sometimes in a hidden way, by souls who have had an authentic encounter with Christ.

Here she sheds light on this new, little-understood vocation discerned and embraced by a growing number of single persons who neither marry nor enter religious life.

These souls are joyfully *single for a greater purpose*, nourishing both the world and the Church with the unique spiritual strengths and graces that God gives to souls who deliberately remain single for Him—in the world but not of it.

In the face of mounting difficulties in our world and our Church, God is now calling for an army of dedicated singles—laymen for the Kingdom of God—nourished from within and empowered by an authentic, personal encounter with Him alone.

Read these pages to learn:

- Why dedicated single life is uniquely suited to our times
- How it builds on our baptismal vocations
- The special role that dedicated singles have in the Church
- How the dedicated-single vocation complements marriage and religious life
- How celibacy for the sake of the Kingdom yields a fruitful spousal relationship with Christ
- How dedicated singles can follow the evangelical counsels of obedience and poverty outside the structured life of a religious community
- The vows that singles can take to dedicate themselves to such service of God within the world

"*Single for a Greater Purpose* is a book that will surely aid the spirituality of those who read it." Cardinal Timothy Dolan

"This book is critical. It also happens to be a rigorous, joyful labor of love and a gift to us. Read it. Pray about it. Discuss it." Kathryn Jean Lopez

"An important and quite beautiful exploration of an underappreciated state of life, written by one who has lived the single vocation with grace and courage, to the benefit of both Church and society." George Weigel

SOPHIA
INSTITUTE PRESS

www.SophiaInstitute.com

ISBN: 978-1-622826-568

51895

9 781622 826568